FOCUS

*Tuning in to your inner guidance
and fulfilling your dreams*

SHARON TAWFILIS M.A.

BALBOA.PRESS
A DIVISION OF HAY HOUSE

Balboa Press books may be ordered through booksellers or by contacting:

Balboa Press
A Division of Hay House
1663 Liberty Drive
Bloomington, IN 47403
www.balboapress.com
844-682-1282

Because of the dynamic nature of the Internet, any web addresses or
links contained in this book may have changed since publication and
may no longer be valid. The views expressed in this work are solely those
of the author and do not necessarily reflect the views of the publisher,
and the publisher hereby disclaims any responsibility for them.

The author of this book does not dispense medical advice or prescribe the use
of any technique as a form of treatment for physical, emotional, or medical
problems without the advice of a physician, either directly or indirectly. The
intent of the author is only to offer information of a general nature to help
you in your quest for emotional and spiritual well-being. In the event you use
any of the information in this book for yourself, which is your constitutional
right, the author and the publisher assume no responsibility for your actions.

Any people depicted in stock imagery provided by Getty Images are
models, and such images are being used for illustrative purposes only.
Certain stock imagery © Getty Images.

Print information available on the last page.

ISBN: 978-1-9822-6126-9 (sc)
ISBN: 978-1-9822-6127-6 (hc)
ISBN: 978-1-9822-6128-3 (e)

Library of Congress Control Number: 2021900282

Balboa Press rev. date: 01/21/2021

This book is dedicated to my son's,

Adam and Gabriel.
May you always follow your hearts.

~ Mom

FOREWORD

I met Sharon 20 years ago when I was teaching dance. She had been on a winding road with lots of bumps and turns and she was still navigating the curvy path to finding herself. Sharon's spirit rose to the top again and again. She maintained a vital resilience, a sense of humor, and a positive outlook on life, even when her life was on painful trajectory. She worked through the grief, anger, and emotional pain to be able to serve others on their path in life, especially when those paths were difficult.

As time passed, our relationship transformed, and the roles of teacher-student swapped many times. Her experiences and *wisdom born from her experiences* were like little gems in my life. I was privileged to get to know her even better when she did over two years of intensive hands-on study with my mom, Donna Eden – a pioneer in the field of Energy Medicine.

At first, I thought Sharon's optimism was a sort of

mask so she wouldn't have to deal with the hard stuff. Was she maintaining an even keel because she was not really dealing with the underbelly of life? No, on the contrary, she reached into the underbelly and wrote *Focus* based on her deepest wisdom, as well as years of study with some of the greatest teachers in the world of self-development and health.

In *Focus*, Sharon helps you, so the mental obstacles, stress, anxiety, and worry don't keep you from greatness. She has spent decades in helping clients, and people from all walks of life eliminate self-judgement and strengthen their self-worth. She gives you all the tools you need so you can change those parts of your life that you desire to change and nurture the ones that you value. She shares lessons, ideas, and successful strategies that some of the greatest spiritual leaders have used to bring physical health, emotional wellness, joy, clarity, and peace to their lives. She gives easy, doable, and practical techniques that can provide powerful trainings to help you blossom and evolve your life to the next level of awareness. Sharon is the perfect partner as she guides you on a transformative journey of healing and to support your personal path.

Shifting your life into an extraordinary one or maintaining a sense of peace in a crazy world is uncomplicated with Sharon inspiring you and motivating you along the way. The techniques in this book are simple, and they are for everyone.

If you want more purpose in life, Sharon shows you how to discover it, so every day is a day of clarity and joy...

If you feel a little lost, Sharon will shine the light so you can find your way and gain focus...

If you find yourself in the most miserable of circumstances with seemingly no way out, Sharon will help you begin to see your path...

If you want to make some meaningful changes, Sharon guides you through the steps to embrace your uniqueness and love whoever and wherever you are in this moment...

If you feel fairly good about your life but you are wanting a sort of awakening to new insight, Sharon can help you start now...

If you have already dug deep into your soul to find meaning, but you need a refresh, Sharon will take you on an insightful and wonderful journey through these pages...

Do not mistake the simplicity of this book. The teachings and exercises are potent and Sharon's depth of sensitivity in her writing will shower you in wisdom that you can utilize immediately. You can bring your desires to fruition.

Philosopher Viktor Frankl says that the motivation for living comes from finding meaning in life and also the freedom to choose one's attitude in any given set of circumstances. He reminds us that when we can no longer change a situation, we are forced to change ourselves. Sharon Tawfilis will help you to make that change that you desire – to deepen the connection to your own soul.

There is always a place in our world for a book like this. And now, more than ever, with important shifts happening on our planet, there is no better time for *Focus.*

Dondi Dahlin, Author of *The Five Elements*
January 2021
San Diego, CA

ACKNOWLEDGEMENTS

I would like to begin by giving credit to high school Psychology teachers. It was in my Psychology class at Patrick Henry High that my interest in Psychology was ignited.

I would like to thank the late Louise Hay whose book, "You Can Heal Your Life" was the first book I read on the subject of and the first time I had heard about, self-healing.

I would like to extend my deepest gratitude to the staff at Thunder Road Adolescent Treatment Centers, Inc. in Oakland Ca., to include Dee Gagnon, Mike Wachter, Nancy, and Elizabeth Escobar who hired me as an intern and brought me into the arena supporting me all the way.

I would like to thank Dr. Bob Lee who studied directly under Carl Rogers for imparting his deep wisdom in teaching me everything he knew about the Person-Centered Approach so I could sit for my license. In addition, his approach to Psychology was my first example of combining Psychology with spirituality.

I would like to thank Laurie Chapman for believing in me and sharing with me important contacts in the field of counseling when I returned to San Diego.

I would like to extend my deepest gratitude to world renowned Donna Eden for following her inner guidance and sharing her wealth of knowledge in the field of Energy Medicine through her school, books and lectures. It was her teachings that I first learned practical applications for an alternative approach to medicine and self-healing.

I would like to thank Sean and Lilian Hodges for taking me into their Ohana at Aloha Psychological Associates, Inc. and for providing both their therapists and clients with a place for all to heal in the spirit of Aloha.

I would like to thank Ashley Lee, BSN RN CCRN Advanced Energy Healer for sharing her healing skills, expertise and vast knowledge in Quantum healing with me and my family.

I would also like to thank all the courageous hearts who have come to my office for counseling over the years and their willingness and vulnerability to open to healing themselves, their marriages and their families.

A special thank you to my dear friend of 35 years, Margrete Chadwick for her friendship and support through all the ups and downs of life and with whom I could speak openly about the process of healing and about things that I didn't always understand and for her patience during the hours of practicing Energy Medicine techniques and energy testing.

Another special thank you to Dondi Dahlin for supporting me and sharing with me her experience and knowledge about the book writing and publishing process and for her dear friendship as well as introducing me to her mother Donna Eden and Energy Medicine, belly dance lessons, and the world of 17th and 18th century costuming!

I would also like to acknowledge and thank all the healers that I received sessions from in my quest to heal and to learn what works for me.

My deepest gratitude goes out to all those who put themselves out into the arena to share their gifts and talents so that everyone may have access to a variety of ways to improve their health and well-being.

INTRODUCTION

There was a time when human beings walked the earth and their sole purpose was merely to survive. We have arrived at such a time that we now have the ability to elevate each and every single human being. We are guided to work together to bring everyone up to the same level. We are doing this now with the help of spiritual beings living ordinary lives. You could already be encountering one of these spiritual beings in your neighbor or your friend without knowing. They are here to guide you. They also have very special purposes in the lives that they have lived. Many have suffered in an effort to release suffering from the planet. They were assigned these sacred human positions before they were born.

This book will describe how we can help ourselves. We are interdependent yet must choose the best path for ourselves. It doesn't have to be difficult to achieve what is our birthright. Love is our birthright. We have placed so many things in the way of this all the while it is the only thing we are looking for. All of us want the same thing regardless of how we go about finding it. Most people would agree that underneath all of the busy-ness, going after wants, struggling in relationships, lies the same core desire that if truly realized would alleviate all of the ills on the planet. That core desire is rooted in love and is to be loved, to experience love.

My hope in writing this book is to provide people with enough evidence about what is being offered to us in as many ways possible, to help us raise our consciousness and stand in conscious choice. My goal is to expose readers to an array of what is out there. I have spent many years researching, at first because I was interested then I became fascinated then it was out of necessity through the pain of my own transformation. It is only a belief that letting go has to be painful or that changing or shifting has to be hard work. It is a belief that is very common and so it is that we go about transforming through pain. This is changing now as we begin to recognize the truth of who we are and that we create how we want to experience ourselves in this human existence. As we practice uncovering our beliefs, we are able to recognize the beliefs that are buried and oftentimes, subtle.

There are many helpers in every community. Those that care for the planet, those that care for animals, those that live in painful situations and in difficult places as well as those that have not experienced a lot of suffering. I say this to bring hope to an ailing human race. Enough of us have asked for help and we now receive the answers to our prayers. Our prayers have been heard and answered. Even if it looks dark around us, even if we don't see hope, there is a purpose for everything. We need to trust that even if we don't understand the actions of others, they could be one of the ones who came here to help. Have you heard the song with the words, "What if God was one of us"?

Ready to evolve?

Exercise:

Write down 3 people that you feel are helpers in your life or in your community.

Who are the people that you notice in your personal life, in your community and beyond? Write them down. It is powerful to see the list as it grows.

I invite you to look around you and ask yourself, "Who is the helper?" You may be surprised to find they aren't the ones you think. We have it all mixed up in our quests to fulfill our longings. It is all breaking down before our very eyes. We are worried yet most of us know it's been a long time coming. The time is now to let go of the chaos we have created and go back to a simpler time. Only we are not going back but forward to the new and improved.

Love informs all of us now. Enough of us have paved the way to allow in what is best for all regardless of race, religion, culture or beliefs. We are one.

Nothing I have said so far hasn't already been said a hundred different times in a hundred different ways. And yet, we are at a place in human history that is unprecedented. We have more war, not less. We have more suffering, not less. We have more money, not less. We have more resources and we are killing ourselves a thousand different ways on a thousand different days.

Many are calling for the end to the senselessness and yet it persists. Many have the knowledge to help us see our way through to healing what needs to be healed, to changing what needs to be changed. These are the helpers. They are wise beyond their years. They call for action, they call for change, in politics, in communities, in schools, in governments, in countries, in cities, in corporations, in churches, in family systems and beyond.

This is a call to action. Yet, all we need to do is to identify the ones already in place, ready to bring forth

God's plan. The helpers are in place. They are ready to do what they have prepared for their entire lives. They have prepared new legislation, new ideas for how to educate our children, peaceful ways to resolve conflict, an appreciation for all ways human beings represent "Being", and, most of all, the true meaning of love and what love truly looks like in human form.

Mr. Rogers did an interview in the 70's where the politicians were moved by his speech calling for children to look for the helpers in a disaster. What we are currently experiencing is a disaster and if Mr. Rogers were here he would be looking for the helpers. They are there.

I don't think many would disagree that our old thinking created what we are currently living. And if we could create that then we could create something else. If we take responsibility, all of us, even if we didn't directly choose this thing or that thing, this attitude or that attitude, we can choose not to align with collective fear, collective doubt, collective grief, a collective sense of injustice, collective regret, collective aggression, collective judgement, collective apathy, and instead there are enough helpers, that we can now join a collective sense of community of forward thinking groups where each individual takes responsibility for how they feel, how they interact, how they heal (the physical and the emotional), and how they love.

I'm not suggesting finding new experts to give our power away to. I am talking about a collective round table where people listen to one another from a place of acceptance and personal empowerment. They are not threatened about the different ways that people see life because each individual has the ability to think and make choices from their own guidance that they trust, to embody and access their higher selves, and therefore need not fear what they may not understand due to a difference in culture, race, religion, or belief. One can access a place of clarity that guides to what is best, and what is right for each individual. Imagine a world where each person listens to the guidance of their higher self, their highest access point to discover what is for the true and highest good for themselves and, at the same time, for the good of all.

It's not possible for too many people to be talking about this. John Lennon wrote the song "Imagine," about this in the 70's. His creative achievement was borne out of his ability to listen to the collective voice of love, the collective longing for a better world where our children are safe and our men and women don't go off to war, and everyone has a voice.

This book is simple to read because truth is not complicated. What is truly important is not complicated. What is real is not complicated. People complicate things in order to cover up. People complicate things to distract. People complicate things to hide. People complicate things so we will not know. People have made things so complicated that we've lost our way. People are buried under layers of individual and collective fear. There is a way out. Everyone has heard it before. The way out is through love.

We just need to learn what love is.

Love is joy.

Love is truth.

Love is community.

Love is help.

Love is kindness.

Love is peace.

Love is gentle.

In love lies the solution.

To every.

Question.

So how do we get there?
ONE PERSON AT A TIME.

(Note: I use the word "God" but it can be interchanged with "Spirit", "the "Divine", "Love" or any other word that is your personal expression of this energy).

TABLE OF CONTENTS

CHAPTER 1

AWARENESS

*The state or condition of being aware;
having knowledge; consciousness.*

What is the purpose of being aware? How can awareness assist us in creating the lives that we want? It is important for all of us to be aware of how we have been conditioned so that we can learn to make conscious choice. If we are not making conscious choice we are allowing outside influences to choose for us.

There is light in all of us. There is light in you. We are all connected to the same light. There isn't different light of different names. You might say luz or lumiere or noor, but it's the same light. You can't put out this light.

"Out beyond right and wrong there is a field,
I will meet you there,"

Rumi.

There have been many guides for decades, in our modern times. And yet, we are still here destroying each other, destroying ourselves. Suicides are at an all-time high. Mass murder has become all too common. It seems that despite everything we know, and all the resources we have, we can't save the lives of school children nor the general public. We can't distribute all the food stores to feed the worlds hungry. All are responsible and in all of us lies the solution.

Who are the helpers?

The helpers are there to assist but the answers already live inside each of us. We know truth when we are in quiet places. We know truth when we slow down. We know truth when we step outside the perceived gates of old structures and step into our own power, our own knowing. The old structures call for someone to be the expert, someone to be above us. Old structures displace our power and keep us needy. This is the result of us having made things complicated. We take for granted that this is the way things are and attempt to mold ourselves to fit in for our own survival.

What if we shift our focus to our higher selves to guide us, in service to US. What if you, upon awakening each day, consciously connect to and embody your higher self and *ask your higher self what it wants you to know? What if you let that inform you what actions to take, how to heal yourself, how to help your community and where to go to discuss what you may not understand knowing that the resulting discussion is helpful to both because neither are the expert. It doesn't mean that we don't need experts. We still need brain surgeons and experts in math, people who know languages and how to teach and people who follow their calling to bring their gifts to the world.*

Even though the answers are simple, it is not simple to do. We need to unravel everything that is preventing us so that we can see what the next step is. You don't have to know in advance the entire journey, as there is no "Guide Book for Modern Times," but merely each next step toward the unfolding of a greater plan. When you relinquish control, you ALLOW the beauty that is waiting for you to burst forth.

When you begin to open your mind to other perspectives, you begin to recognize that you can let go of any false beliefs you once believed to be true about yourself. Your false beliefs about yourself "feel" different than when you "know" something is true. When you practice this exercise, you learn how to "feel" truth and to trust your knowing. What are your beliefs? Many of your beliefs may live in the unconscious and inform much of how you feel. You may feel confused because these feelings may not make sense in your current circumstances or in your current relationships. You may be creating conflict without knowing why.

Ready to evolve?

Exercise: Think of a situation that currently feels heightened for you that has to do with another person. Think of all the perspectives.

 Write down your perspective. Write down the perspective of the others involved.

 (Some people forget to include their perspective in the issue while others forget to consider the perspectives of others – both are valuable)

 Notice what changes for you when considering all perspectives.

---

* I invite you to notice in your daily life when the situation calls for multiple perspectives. You may be are afraid to look and don't realize how you will feel better and your life circumstances and relationships will improve when you do look. It doesn't cost anything to stop judging. It doesn't cost anything to change your beliefs. It doesn't cost anything to entertain new ideas or new ways of being and the old ones will still be there to go back to if you choose. However, what is the cost of suffering in silence, of keeping the status quo, of sticking to what you know because you are not sure what is in the unknown. You may not trust that there is a better way or that you deserve to have your dreams come true. You*

may have hope. You may pray. You go to work. You may not trust that your prayers will be answered. Therefore, you may continue in your same routines and push aside what makes you uncomfortable instead of seeking to uncover your most precious gifts that you came here to share from the purest essence of your being-ness.

Love responds when you ask for what you want. It is important that you know what you want. There is a place where you can access the highest guidance available to you. There are various ways to reach this access point. Meditation is one way to gain access. There are different forms of meditation. Some people prefer to sit and others find a meditative state through more active forms such as yoga, running the vacuum, or gardening. Another way to get into contact with your point of access is to release self-judgments in the unconscious by finding your best way to access these inner workings.

I help my clients do this in therapy in guiding each person to notice themes of emotions and patterns of thought. They are arrows pointing to the stuck places that ultimately are the cause of our suffering. Since we are good at covering up and pushing away we struggle to gain the awareness about what is going on inside ourselves as we create situations and relationships based on these stuck energies. We then blame what is going wrong or what is going right on these situations and relationships. We neither take responsibility nor take credit for what we have created. We are a microcosm of the macrocosm. Just like the weather, we may think life is just happening to us and we have no control over it. We can prepare for the storm, we can find shade in the sun, but we cannot stop the weather from changing. This point of view is outdated. More is available to us now than ever. Mental, emotional, physical and spiritual resources of all kinds are available to us in ways not previously available. Older generations did not have accessibility to what we have today. Therefore, to rely on old ways of doing things is in many cases mistaken. Marianne Williamson so eloquently elucidated how our country is just now beginning to mature as we experience tragedy after tragedy, we are beginning to wake up! We are no longer in the naivete of our youth.

CHAPTER 2

TRANSFORMATION

The state of being transformed.
Change in form, appearance,
nature or character.

*H*ave you noticed any shifts in your life? Have you noticed people or circumstances shifting in the lives of those around you? We are shifting away from old thought patterns which include lack, struggle, victim and perpetrator mentalities, lack of self-worth, fear of the unknown and a focus on money to the detriment of our families. Many don't realize that we are not living a life that was created merely from the conditioning of the present family, but also from ancestors. The world was a very *different place when they created thought patterns and beliefs that are now outdated.*

Things are moving more quickly than ever before. We are being asked, as a result of what we have created, to open ourselves to the miracle that is right in front of us in our own lives. Each one of us has our own story to tell regardless of how we have lived our life. We are all contributing to the masterpiece of this world. To say some contributions are more important than others is false. All actions and reactions have ripple effects throughout humanity. This is why it is so important to acknowledge how all are affected by legislation so that we take care of those that, even though they don't have money, are contributing to the evolution of the planet.

We need all of us to express all the hidden parts to illuminate the dark places. It is in this illumination where we find our freedom. For many of us there is happiness from the beginning of our lives. But many suffer without ever knowing happy moments. This tells us that there are parts of our collective self that are being ignored. When we have eradicated all judgement about ourselves and others will we afford ourselves the ability to release suffering. People may come from the viewpoint such dreams do not exist; however, that is a mistake. If we don't first see it then we cannot bring it forward into being. If people had been asked if it was possible for human beings to fly high in the sky before airplanes were invented, they would have said that it is impossible. However, some saw it first which allowed it to come into being.

> *"All we have to do from this day is dream a new dream."*
>
> *Martin Luther King*

Some are seeing our new world and helping bring forth the new dream. They are the helpers. It is necessary to invite the help utilizing freedom of choice. Help must be beckoned. We can ask to be shown what action to take on the issue at hand. It may be something within that needs to be addressed or it may be a situation calling for a new way. Some believe prayer is the only way to God. God empowers us simply from the asking. God answers us when we take action, on behalf of the greater good. Eventually, for those who are answering the call, we will all be choosing from our highest access point.

It is necessary that we rise above the matrix to which we run our current programming. The old software was created by outdated thinking which has been upgraded as a result of our prayers and the longing in our hearts. For those who are called, updates have been happening around the globe. While all may not know exactly what it means for their own life, as more and more folks choose to listen to inner guidance more, in time they will see. More and more people are waking up as a result of downloading the new. Eckhart Tolle entitled his book "A New Earth" indicating what is coming. He is a helper. Oprah interviews helpers on multitudes of subjects and assists in the illumination. I am a helper. I have helped clear difficult low vibration programs from my family. How are you being called? In your job? Through your health? As a struggle with depression or anger? Financially? Spiritually? People who are homeless are doing their part too and everyone in between has an important part to play in the great unfolding of the evolution of consciousness.

Enough of us are following our inner guidance that real changes are coming quickly. All of this may seem strange to speak about in such a way, but we will grow accustomed to seeing life in fluid and ever-changing ways. As we learn to trust our guidance we become less and less afraid of the unknown and more willing to trust in the absence of proof. It has, until now, seemed an impossibility to truly embrace the kind of love required for this seemingly impossible dream to manifest. Many are dreaming this into being. They are the ushers of light bringing into being the impossible dream. Such help is the proof we have all been asking for. We want proof and we don't recognize the proof. We continue on the path of fear when what we have been asking for has been given.

One helper, Paul Luftenegger, teaches on peace and was asked to perform for the United Nations International Day of Peace. He embodies the answer for which we have asked "How do we move towards world peace?" He reminds us that The Universal Declaration of Human Rights was adopted by the United Nations in December of 1948 yet we have still not fully implemented its doctrine. What is it going to take for us to rectify this? Most folks cannot fathom how they can make such huge changes that will ultimately have an impact on world issues. The purpose of this discussion is to shed light on the solution. Individuals make up the solution by going within and healing, seeking empowered guidance and taking guided action. It is simple and at the same time not simple. Not everyone is motivated to look within for the sake of world peace. We must trust in the order of things that as all unfolds it is truly a part of a greater purpose.

Another helper, Christie Sheldon, is dreaming into existence "Love or Above" based on the research by David Hawkins. David Hawkins created a scale which corresponds each emotional state with a number on a scale. Christie Sheldon has a vision of helping each one of us raise our vibration to 500 or higher which is the equivalent to Love. According to David Hawkins, above a certain emotional state (approximately 200), we begin to contribute to the greater good.

There are helping platforms such as, Mindvalley and AwakeTV which provide a way for seekers to access all kinds of teachings on self-development. Easily accessible online as well as in person courses are offered around the world. Many are those who see the importance not only for themselves but for everyone to create a better world.

We don't have to look far for this kind of support and education. Those with vision are building places for us to gather, gathering at places for us to learn, learning new ways of thinking and thinking into being this new earth! Everyone is called to find their true nature within.

In addition to human helpers, we have the arts to help us awaken. Creative minds are equally important in the movement of consciousness. Looking at a painting or a sculpture can serve to awaken joy and inspiration by touching in a person a place that is not guarded. Listening to music elicits emotion through the vibration of the music and words. The written word is a powerful thing. Words are our most familiar way of exchanging ideas. One day we will be able to "feel" a person's meaning and trust our instincts without proof of spoken and written word. This method of communication already exists between couples, siblings and friends who finish one another's sentences, pick up the phone to call someone only to find they are already calling and feel a strong emotion that is not related to anything happening in their day only to find that someone close to them was feeling that exact emotion.

We are growing in our abilities to sense if someone is telling us the truth or lying. We can make mistakes by going into fear which blocks our knowing. This is why the inner work is so important--so that we don't make mistakes. We place blame outside of ourselves when things don't go according to what we think we want. We don't recognize our responsibility and prejudice in both the outcome and our perception of the outcome. It is our focus that produces the results whether lovingly guided or rooted in fear. Thinking is the channel through which most of our choices are made. Therefore, paying attention to our thoughts teaches us how to know when we are listening to fear or not. It is a skill that can be learned. Paying attention to places in the body that hold energy can help one to know if the emotions they are experiencing are fear.

Louise Hay offered us a complete dictionary of the cause for our ailments in her book "You Can Heal Your Life," introducing the concept that our physical problems are rooted in fear/suppressed emotions and therefore the solution is to release fear/suppressed emotions. Our unconscious beliefs are the driving force behind creating through fear. The issues that we focus on point to what is ready to be released. Christie Sheldon offers a playful way to address what comes up by saying to herself, "Oh! What is this? What do I get to clear today?" and suggests this playful approach instead of judging ourselves for how we feel. When we go into fear we are afraid that how we feel will have a direct effect on whether or not we will get what we want therefore we tend to judge ourselves instead of remaining neutral and curious.

Ready to evolve?

Exercise: Ask yourself "What do I get to clear today?".
Write down what comes up for you.

13

We feel alone despite millions of people sharing the planet with us. We judge ourselves into loneliness creating the exact thing we fear. The book entitled "The Secret" points exactly to this phenomenon while giving direction to how to create what we do want. Help is all around us. We don't have to be "New Age" or have religious leanings or a certain kind of spirituality to benefit from the help that is being offered around us. There are many different approaches offered for as many personal expressions. You can go to church but it doesn't only happen in church. You can be liberal or conservative, but it doesn't only come through that mentality. All of us are called as we are all a part of the whole. We need all of us to come together to lift the planet out of what we are currently experiencing. If each of us every morning asked to be guided throughout our day and followed that guidance we would see rapid change. We take for granted freedom of choice believing life "happens." We are powerful creators and consequently have ultimate responsibility for what has been created. Our world, our country is a direct result of our creations. We are responsible. Love is the foundation for the best possible result.

We can use our voice to lift the world. Each voice sings a song of love. Ultimately, we cannot change who we truly are but when we go into doubt we separate ourselves from the truth of who we are. When we doubt we deprive ourselves from receiving that which is meant for us. From doubt stems fearful action that had doubt not been there, this fearful action would not have been taken. Pay attention in your own daily routine and notice if and when you take an action that was born in doubt. We move so fast in our day to day that we don't notice what drives decisions and actions. We think life "happens" instead of taking responsibility for what we are creating.

From fear we produce doubt, which leads to lessons. If we don't recognize our lessons as opportunities we erode our trust and faith. We want proof and when we get it we don't recognize it. Proof looks different than we believe it should look. It isn't the car we have always wanted or the perfect looking family as evidenced by the photos we post on social media or getting the most accolades. It looks like more peace in our daily living absent of the drama and trauma we create when we live unconscious patterns out in the world. We feel satisfied and fulfilled while growing and learning in life and all its imperfection. We love and don't judge how others love. We live and don't judge how others live. We strive to be better people all the while accepting ourselves exactly as we are. Joy becomes a common occurrence and isn't reserved only for special occasions. It is in walking your dog on a beautiful day and witnessing the miracle in a friend's life when they get that "aha!" moment and you get to share it with them. It is in seeing your children work something out for themselves that they were struggling with. It is in looking at the ocean at night and imagining the vastness before you. It is in releasing yourself from the ties that bound you to old family patterns only to find that

15

you always were "OK." Love is present in all you do if you allow it.

Stillness produces the ability to go deep. When you go deep you gain access to profound truth and wisdom to help guide your way. Everyone who decides to engage in a process of self-discovery would appreciate to get through the uncomfortable parts with as much grace as possible. Guidance brings Grace.

When you transform your life, you are following your guidance towards the fulfillment of your purpose. As a result, you begin to notice all types of abundance showing up in a variety of ways.

Abundance is all around you. There is enough for all. Earth's resources are finite but the abundance of the universe is infinite. There are changes that we can make so that every person has healthy food. There are helpers focused on sustainable farming, healthy eating habits and the promotion of food in general which helps us to have options for what we choose to eat. Each one of us cannot possibly specialize in everything but we can honor each person's contribution through what they choose to focus on by paying attention to what they are saying. Each helper in doing their calling is contributing to the transformation of the planet and of humanity towards sustainable living, honoring all people and the planet.

Wayne Dyer taught about the concepts of self-responsibility. He learned across his lifetime through trial and error. People such as he and countless others have paved the way for us so that we don't have to spend our entire lifetime searching for answers. When we humble ourselves, and stop thinking that we know, we open the gate for our learning. Following your inner guidance is how you change the world. Since the beginning of time, we have strived merely to survive in a seemingly hostile environment. Protecting ourselves from harsh elements, trying to stay fed and constantly learning new ways to improve our circumstances has led us on this ever-evolving road to seeking more and better. We don't seem to know when to stop or slow down. The younger generations will be the change-makers in such areas as corporate and other systems. They are already making headway in many areas. Attention has been put towards childcare, outdoor break spaces, exercise and providing easy access to healthy food options. More time spent away from work is needed as has already been commonplace in most European countries. Love is the foundation of all decisions, all actions, all stories about life, all circumstances and relationships when guidance is followed. Teach how to access and follow guidance and peace will follow. Learn the true meaning of love and it will be easier to know what following your intuition feels like. Guidance and intuition are related. You need to be familiar with your own intuition to know when you are truly being guided by love and not standing in fear.

Marianne Williamson has been paving the way for conscious politics in our country in recent years. Recently, she wrote "America's defense budget this year will be 718

Billion, a number that has less to do with the necessary expenditure to provide for America's safety and more to do with the financial gain to the US defense industry, or what Eisenhower called the "military industrial complex". Meanwhile, America's enemies arrive less by land, air, or sea than they do through the internet. One day, if humanity is to survive, we will reformulate our notion of security. We will make peace building measures such as restorative justice, conflict resolution, the eradication of poverty, the expansion of economic opportunity particularly to women, and the universality of education for the children of the world – as well as meditation and mindfulness – the primary factors in our creation of a sustainable and peaceful world. We will realize that it's as important to wage peace as it is to prepare for war."

You see, we don't have to invent the wheel. If everyone follows their calling, all will be tended to. It may not be your calling to discuss politics or fight for the environment and that is ok. What is most important is that you follow your heart. Marianne speaks from her heart and is following her spiritual/political calling. If we but recognize this as such it is enough. Then we follow our guidance. Marianne is a helper.

There are many helpers behind the scenes as well. True unsung heroes who are helping in ways big and small. You don't have to know who all the helpers are but merely recognize some. In recognizing, you become one of them. Once you recognize, you have attained a certain level of awareness. It is in the recognition that your focus is turned to what is truly important. You can have differing views on many things, but the underlying basic tenets will be the same. Equality, dignity, justice, are but a few of the basics that are not even questioned once a particular level of awareness is reached, they just come naturally. Justice is not an issue in a society when all are treated equal and you have completely let go of victim/perpetrator programming. High functioning doesn't just look like the corporate CEO or the successful physician or lawyer. High functioning is not inherent in particular vocations. What we consider to be successful is rapidly changing. "Happy is the new rich." You can be an accomplished athlete, but still have difficulty finding true happiness as we have witnessed in some courageous athletes who have come forward in their stories of depression and anxiety and how they chose to face themselves in order to overcome these issues. Facing yourself can feel daunting if you are in fear. You may think you will have to give up your lifestyle to which you are attached or a habit you are comfortable with and fear you won't know how or can't. Many fear change. We fear people and circumstances won't change and at the same time we fear they will. It doesn't cost anything to change a belief. If you change the belief that you are not worthy to you are worthy, you will have everything to gain and nothing to lose. Your thought patterns will reset and your energy systems will go into better balance. You will create changes in yourself down to the cellular level. You have more influence over what happens in your life than you realize. What you focus on grows.

What do you want more of in your life? If you focus on lack you will have more lack. If you can't help but focus on lack and you know this is not helping, then you know that there is something in your unconscious that needs your attention. People don't purposely try to sabotage their own happiness. They just need help finding hidden beliefs, childhood wounding and consequent suppression of feelings and fears so that they can free themselves from triggers, unconscious behavior patterns, unconscious thought patterns. It is common to think that you know what happened in your past and you are where you are now and not there, but in reality, the past is alive in the present in your ongoing issues. Many think that their issues are due to people and circumstances but those are just mirrors to what you need to look at in yourself. People get so invested in their story that they don't want to let go of it before they get the result that they have been wanting and waiting for. To let go of the false belief before receiving the desired outcome is difficult to imagine. Regret is a common reaction to the realization that one has spent years focusing on the wrong things or in the wrong ways.

"When you know better you do better."
Maya Angelou

If you could but trust that the universe conspires to give you that which you want as is so eloquently stated in Paolo Coelho's, "The Alchemist," you could release what stands in the way of your receiving. In so doing, you help all of humanity to rise. You have gifts to give your communities and the world. Releasing everything that is in your unconscious is not a prerequisite to sharing yourself and all that you have to offer, however, this level of giving is difficult to balance when you are encumbered by your past. It comes more easily and smoothly when you are not draining your energy due to people and circumstances that are there to show you what you need to pay attention to within yourself.

> *"Everything changes when you start to emit your own frequency rather than absorbing the frequencies around you, when you start imprinting your intent on the universe rather than receiving an imprint from existence."*

> *Wild Woman Sisterhood (Instagram)*

> *Ready to evolve?*
>
> *Exercise: Write down your centering theme for the day.*
> *Ask yourself "What do I want to feel today?" Allow what comes to mind even if you don't think you can feel this way. Take a few minutes to imagine and invite in this feeling. Throughout the day when you think of it, remind yourself of your centering them and bring back the feeling of it.*

When you see your challenges with people and circumstances for what they are, it is much easier to change how you view them. Some are there to show you what you need to pay attention to in yourself. When you realize this, you can choose to no longer go into agreement with the projections of others, for example. This can be challenging when we are speaking about deeply ingrained family patterns and long histories of projected stories that were put on you, but this is much easier to separate from once you recognize what it is. We may want to try to help or try to fix others but cannot help or fix outside of our own actions and behaviors. We can live our lives free of the old rules therefore showing others that there is another way. We cannot choose for them as they must choose for themselves based on their own journey and their own calling. People often rebut obvious changes in a family member's ways of living as a result of feeling threatened. They make excuses for their judgments feeling justified in their attacks. If they could see that their reactions are sign posts for what is needed for their internal healing they would discontinue their negative projections. This is what makes it so difficult for us to change what isn't working by holding each other down with projections that are not based in love. Emoto's experiments with water showed that by simply placing a word next to water it would change its "shape." In essence, projecting an intention on water causes water to take shape based on the intention. Our bodies are made up of a large amount of water.

Making the changes that would change the world doesn't have to be complicated. You just need to pay attention to yourself, to how you are feeling, to what upsets you, to what causes you pain and recognize all of it for what it is. When you recognize the small things that upset you in your daily life as something other than happening to you – you do your part in creating world peace. There IS something you can do that WILL have profound impact. This has been said in so many different ways but there can't be too many of us saying the same thing because we come from so many different styles and walks of life. We have complicated everything in ways that life doesn't need. We have created so much competition in order to survive and meet basic needs. This takes each of us away from following our passion, our calling.

Your calling is always in service to "US." So much of what has been written and spoken about in popular circles involves following your passion in order to have an abundant life and this may feel selfish or self-centered to some. But when you follow your calling and usher in abundance into your life, you are lifting yourself up in every way changing the landscape of your life and those around you. You are raising the vibration of the planet and helping everyone. When you raise yourself up you cannot help but follow your guidance and do your part in service to others. When you are no longer striving and surviving, you have space in your life and space in your heart unencumbered and open, you walk with tremendous support to fulfill the path that is laid before you. This is the most sacred path, to follow the path of love. This could be confused as it has been throughout history, with what is the righteous path. After all, love doesn't just lay down and accept everything as it is given especially when it is obvious that actions are being taken that have nothing to do with love. This is why you, having presence of mind about your own issues as well as in the practice of following divine guidance, will take right action each step along the path.

"If you are not in the arena, also getting your ass kicked, I am not interested in your feedback"

Brene Brown

CHAPTER 3

HEAR

To listen to; give or pay attention to.

"The Voice" by Shel Silverstein

There is a voice inside of you
That whispers all day long,
"I feel that this is right for me,
I know that THIS is wrong."
No teacher, preacher, parent, friend
Or wise man can decide
What's right for you–just listen to
The voice that speaks inside.

Y*ou will make mistakes. This is the beauty of being human. And through your mistakes you will deepen* *your connection to yourself and to the divine. Your mistakes become natural guideposts to ensure that you do not overlook, you do not distract, you do not complicate, and you do not hide. You don't want to fall into the trap of perfectionism or thinking that you "know" all the time. Life is a magnificent and continuous unfolding.*

> *"Organically, the release of "fear of the unknown" happens, when we actively choose on a daily basis, to embody the awareness of having trust and faith in the absence of proof."*
>
> *Ashley Lee*
> *RN, BSN, CCRN Advanced energy healer.*

Ready to evolve?

Exercise: Identify a situation that you are having difficulty having trust and faith in that it will work out.

Write it down.

Ask yourself if there is a next step you can take in creating what you want and write it down.

Tell yourself; "I ask for this or something better and so it is".

In what do you place your tender heart in faith? With whom do you place your loving trust? Some refer to God, some call it the universe or universal spiritual truth, but whatever you refer to, there must be a sense of a loving creator. When you listen to the call of your heart you discover the particular ways in which you connect to your existence. Many people have spiritual beliefs based in religion, some formed out of the sense of wonder about how nature was created and continues to form and thrive each day, yet others experience God through their love for God's children experiencing in every smile and every embrace the sense of purpose for which you were created. We need to stop making others wrong for their different perceptions. We are being invited to release the idea that we are separate.

More than ever, we are being given examples as beacons of undeniable proof that all the things that we previously used as excuses for separation were undeniably false. Some families are experiencing having children who are born a particular gender and are proclaiming they are a different gender shaking their family to the core. People dedicated to old fashioned religious beliefs are being stretched after finding out that their children are not heterosexual. This is not to punish or isolate anyone, it is to show human beings that LOVE is LOVE. IT illuminates the preposterousness that LOVE could be anything else than meant for every being. To say that you are not worthy of love because you are black or white, or straight or gay, or born in a body that is the opposite of how you feel inside is to most humans undeniably false

27

SHARON TAWFILIS M.A.

in this day and age. We know better and, "when we know better we do better," (Maya Angelou). We do better now!

EVERYONE wants to be loved. If they lash out about differences there is something in each one of them that is crying out to be healed. The worse the behavior the worse the fear and the more love that is needed. There isn't a guide book for how to handle the worst situations on the planet, but there is a day to day solution which is for each of us to follow our higher guidance. If you connect to your higher self and your highest access point there is no reason why you cannot heal this planet of all the old, unnecessary, outdated, beliefs and consequent lifestyles that you have taken for granted as "the way it is."

People who fight for there to be no change do so out of fear. There is something in them that tells them there is danger in change, danger in the unknown. Unaware, these people go into alert anytime they suspect a threat. What constitutes a threat depends on factors including where you live, what generation you are from, socio-economic status, level of education, how you were raised, and beliefs and perceptions about life and relationships. But, regardless of what constitutes a threat for change, it is still a threat. The ego steps in and as its job is protector, raises the alarm.

Pronoia is a term meaning the opposite of paranoia. It means that the universe is conspiring in our favor. This spiritual wisdom can lift resistance to change. It is the solution to the fear that we will not get what we want. The dreams in our hearts have divine purpose.

28

You are not wrong for wanting the life that you want. Wanting what you want is one way that the universe gets your attention steering you in the direction it is trying to lead you towards a happy and fulfilling life, if that is what you are asking for. This is, in large part, the reason why our linear minds cannot fathom the unfolding of most things. The universe fashions your life circumstances like weaving together cloth, one thread at a time. The resulting fabric is a work of art and love designed to illuminate the world of spirit and its presence in your life. It is proof that you are not alone and the universe is on your side. When you witness good coming to others you may celebrate their good fortune as another example of what is meant for all of us. This doesn't mean you sit on the couch while the universe gets to work. You co-create the design of the fabric as a result of listening to the call of your heart.

We generally cannot grasp how we are being helped to get to where we want to go. Your life may take twists and turns you never would have expected all because the universe is listening to what you are saying you want. It is always listening. Language is critical in how you communicate. Paying attention to what you say and making changes to the language you choose cultivates self-responsibility. It is the result of being mindful about your thoughts. Trust and faith can create a huge shift in your life. If you feel a resistance to changing your thoughts you can make it a temporary change, see how it goes and then go back to your old ways if you feel it is not serving you.

If you are not at the place of making the change in action then you know there is a next step for you before the change comes. It may be uncovering a belief that is preventing you from seeing clearly. You may be invested in this belief and want to hold on tight. You held on because of the promise of this belief or you may be buying into old messages such as, "you can't teach an old dog new tricks."

Investment is another reason why you may have resistance. How can you simply "let go" of something you have been holding on to for many years, even decades? You had your reasons for these beliefs so, how can you simply say that now you don't have these beliefs anymore? Your identity and life purpose may have become entangled and now you are left wondering who you really are. You may find new purpose in allowing yourself to be guided. It is a muscle you grow with practice. It requires concentration and focus. It is available to everyone. It is important to not compare yourself to other people you know because everyone has their own way of going about it. An important daily practice everyone can incorporate is to pay attention to your own judgments about how people should act, conduct their lives, be in relationship, be in the world, and handle all the areas of their lives. I have heard this said many times before and it is worth saying again, "we have no idea what is going on in people's lives." We really don't know since people are affected mentally, emotionally, physically and spiritually by their own issues as well as other factors. If you truly want to understand someone you can choose to "be with" them with all the conditions present as defined by the late Psychologist Carl Rogers. Carl Rogers defined specific conditions that when present in the relationship, elicits healing change.

These conditions are:

1) *Two persons are in psychological contact.*
2) *The first, whom we shall term the client, is in a state of incongruence, being vulnerable or anxious.*
3) *The second person, whom we shall term the therapist, is congruent or integrated in the relationship.*
4) *The therapist experiences unconditional positive regard for the client.*
5) *The therapist experiences an empathic understanding of the client's internal frame of reference and endeavors to communicate this experience to the client.*
6) *The communication to the client of the therapist's empathic understanding and unconditional positive regard is to a minimal degree achieved. You can replace "the therapist," with "the parent," "the friend," "the Pastor," "the Rabbi," "the police officer," "the teacher," "the senator," etc.*

Guidance is available to you from your higher self and from folks who can offer the conditions as defined by Carl Rogers. It is important to note that guidance does not come in the form of "expert" advice but from loving awareness and listening with these conditions.

Change is less complicated than you may realize. A common myth is that it must be hard work or a challenge to be worthwhile. In the past, change took a long time but we don't have to run that program anymore. You can uncover and illuminate and change can happen at that very moment. You can release what was once hidden in your unconscious the moment you shine light on it. You can change an old habit right away. We have those who have come before us and paved the way, when it wasn't popular to do so, to thank for the opportunities that we have now. There are also folks who are pioneering ahead for the times we live in now.

I recently saw a segment on the news about a police officer who is bringing meditation to the police force. He was clear to state, that he didn't want to be some hippie guy just a police officer who has found value in meditation to help him with his work, who wants to spread this awareness to his fellow officers on the force around the country stating that incidences of aggression decrease when officers are in the practice of mindfulness. This police officer took a big chance and went out on a limb to bring something, that was formerly not considered masculine nor appropriate, to a very masculine entrenched system. What they found is that it has been helpful for the officers. In the past we would not have thought of a police officer in spiritual terms but that was our old thinking. The helpers come in all forms. They are found in every area of life, even places we would not have normally expected. This is why we cannot simply look in the traditional places for answers to our human issues but rather look for those who can provide the person-centered conditions when we are looking for outside help.

We have witnessed systems that are in place fail to live up to their designated assignments 100 percent of the time. There are helpers in every area of life by design. They are helpers, not experts. We are shifting away from the Matriarchal, Patriarchal, Hierarchical programs and ways of seeing society to the inclusive "Service to Us." You can seek help and you are a part of the solution and now are guided to feel into it to see if it feels right to you before blindly taking advice, including in our healthcare. We historically built a system of experts with whom we placed our trust. We now recognize that we are our own experts. We can make informed choices with the help of trusted advisors who do not claim to know what is best for us, but merely can offer specialized knowledge that we add to the decision-making process. Carl Rogers was the first to do this in the field of psychology. He suggested that the client is the expert in his or her story and the therapist is the student in learning their story while providing the 6 conditions. People every day are taking charge of their children's healthcare by deciding what is right for their family. They are not simply following popular protocol. Some families are choosing to homeschool or are working to change the structure of education. Many individuals are choosing to not have children. People are listening to their inner voice in ways we did not do in the past. We have moved up Maslow's hierarchy of needs and now we have more choices. We have the luxury to think for ourselves and not be punished or ostracized or left out in any way. We have a responsibility to exercise this freedom that was bought and paid for by those who have paved the way and continue to pave the way. They are the helpers.

The greatest joy we will find is to pass along the gifts each of us carries inside. The way that you access these gifts, if you are not already in touch with them, is to listen to your inner guidance. Pay attention to what comes to the forefront in your gestalt. That is what is beckoning you to investigate in yourself and in your life.

If you have "Pronoia" you will have faith and trust that your experiences are in your favor and that you are exactly where you need to be. You are being supported because you are a part of the greater cause for the betterment of humanity. Your contributions are vastly important to the weaving of the fabric of the best possible society for our time. Many of us feel that life is too busy to follow your passion or to be creative. An example that comes to mind is the two moms who started making funny videos about parenting (IMOMSOHARD) and are now traveling around the country performing for audiences. They are being paid to bring joy and humor about the mundane parts of parenting to countless parents dealing with the same thing and they get to do what brings THEM joy! They are having fun!

I imagine that if someone had asked them if they have the time to do what they are doing now, they would have said absolutely not!

Another great example of someone who listened to her inner voice is Lisa Nichols. Lisa is an internationally renowned motivational speaker, published author, and successful entrepreneur. One of her motivational speeches can be found on Youtube. She describes how she went from being a single working parent who didn't have money for milk and diapers and turned her life into something most folks probably would not have imagined by listening to her inner guidance that she could do it even though she didn't have proof in the moment. She is now doing what she loves to do and has financial security.

Christie Sheldon teaches her students to open up their ideas about where money can come from. Money can come from a traditional paycheck but money can also come through many different channels therefore it is important not to be closed to money coming through a variety of ways.

When you listen to your inner guidance, you learn what it is that you truly want and find access for how to get there. When you listen to get information about next steps, each next step will be given to you as you listen and follow your inner guidance.

> *Ready to evolve?*
>
> *Exercise: Contemplate and then write down 2 new possibilities for a stream of income that you had not previously considered.*

CHAPTER 4

"PRONOIA"

*a neologism which means the
opposite of paranoia. All the world
is conspiring in my favor.*

*I*s there anything that you have noticed in your own life
that seemed to just work out in an unexpected way? To
quote Melissa McCarthy, has anything happened that you
made you feel you "got hit with the lucky stick"?

There are things that I have noticed in my life recently
that feel they have come to resolution in miraculous ways.
Things that are working like writing this book, insights
that my children are having, and job opportunities not
previously considered. I started meditating on all the
miracles that have happened. They kept accumulating even

when I thought I had thought of everything. It is a miracle that I feel joy most days and am excited to wake up in the morning. People seem to receive me in new ways where I feel seen. Seeing my clients with deep clarity without having to make an effort and have that reflected back to me when they connect deeply to my understanding of them, is my honor to witness. Enjoying myself regardless of who is around is a miracle. Trusting that my children have all the help they need is a blessing I do not take for granted. These are the types of things that have caught my focus and they are very different from what I frequently focused on in the past.

In the past, my focus was often from a place of fear. I had thought patterns which I had created in my childhood that were not true but that I would use to assess situations in my adult life and make decisions which had negative effects on most areas of my life. I had all of the most common roadblocks to success. When we create our lives standing in fear it sends messages out into the universe about what we believe and the universe responds accordingly. This concept from the popular book "The Secret" has been well described. To put into action, it is necessary to lovingly release the fear from its position of creating in our lives.

Fear/ego wants to prove to us that it is right. The problem is that what it believes is not true. It stands in the way of your receiving what you want to receive. This part of yourself creates from fear. When you give it love and with conviction state, "You are no longer in charge, I am," you empower yourself by recognizing that you control your mind, it does not control you. It may be necessary to continue to remind this part of yourself that it is not in charge. You want to consciously create when standing in Love. When you consciously create from Love, you are in "Service to Us." When you create in Service to Us, you create what is the best for yourself and everyone involved. Things happen with ease when you recognize you have support and follow your guidance. Support and guidance are always there when decisions are made from Love.

So often you may feel you are completely on your own trying to get things done. The difference lies in whether or not you are forcing something to happen or going with the flow. Going with the flow doesn't mean you don't have work to do. It means you are following your instincts and going where you are guided or engaging with work you feel inspired to do so it doesn't feel as much like work as when you are trying to "make" something happen. The universe doesn't require you to work day and night and make yourself ill from lack of sleep or from being out of balance in order for miracles to occur. We have bought into the old myth that the harder we work, the more successful we will be. The harder we work, the more we will have and the more we have the more successful we are. We are turning a corner with new mantras trending such as "Happy is the new rich". We have recognized that too much sacrifice accumulating wealth lowers our quality of life and distracts us from deepening our awareness of self.

You are here to grow in self-awareness and are called to uncover what is in the unconscious as well as find your unique gifts and talents that you came here to share with the world and especially with those closest to you. Through these pathways you may extend yourself in love and contribute to making the world a better place. It requires a new focus than what you have previously been accustomed for those of us who still have the old programming. This doesn't mean that it's not good to create financial abundance. In general, you aren't meant to suffer and be uncomfortable unless there is something important you are learning in that state. Generally, your calling will include a way to feed and house you if not more creature comforts. You may be called to create wealth in the beginning of your life and then move on to something else later. There is no end to the possibilities and possible outcomes to how you can express love through the life you live. The money you have may play an important role or it may have nothing to do with your lessons or the expression of your gifts in the world. Every expression is different just like every person is different. Every expression is woven into the tapestry of Love's expression of Life.

We outsource everything in our modern world. It is becoming more and more popular to eat out or have food delivered and cook less. We pay for things to be done for us more than we ever have before. There is one thing that cannot be done for us that we might ignore until we can't ignore it anymore or simply choose not to and that is to raise our own consciousness. It's an inside job. People can help but unless you are willing no amount of help can do it for you. It's perfectly ok to go in kicking and screaming if that is how you feel. It's not necessary to be in complete surrender. All you need to do is show up regardless of how pissed off, hurt or numb you are. You don't have to feel a certain way to successfully elicit growth. It may take some time before you start feeling different or you may feel a sense of relief or a new sense of direction right away.

You may go from one healer, teacher, or guide to the next as you grope in the dark not knowing where any of this is taking you. You may doubt the validity or the necessity of venturing out on your spiritual or psychological path fearing it won't go anywhere and you will be mocked by family and friends. Then suddenly you wake up one morning and remember that you used to feel a certain way that you scarcely remember feeling but you know that you weren't as happy or as peaceful as you are now. It may sneak up on you and slowly you feel less and less anxious until you forget how anxious you used to be.

You may find that you are able to reduce depression or anxiety and no longer need the medication you once needed. If you once felt depressed or low energy you may start to feel a little more energy each day then eventually realize that you have started to enjoy your life more. You may find yourself accepting invitations or participating in activities you may have previously denied because you didn't have the energy. When you have more energy, you find more enjoyment in the life you have. You will spend less time on the usual distractions. If you used to have a glass of wine or two every evening, you may find you are not reaching for that anymore. If you spent too many hours working, you may find yourself coming home enjoying more quality time with delighted family members. The shifts and changes are often subtle but over time profound and life altering. Each small decision made is cash in the bank. Deposits are made in the bank of self-awareness towards creating the life you truly want instead of the life you think you must settle for due to conscious and unconscious beliefs.

When you decide to increase self-awareness or work on raising your own consciousness it is usually because of one of a few reasons. You have become open due to being in pain, you want to educate yourself, or you are having an existential crisis. Imagine if it was part of the school curriculum instead of something that is thrown in after a disaster. If we require our children to spend a large amount of time attending school to prepare them for life why not include courses on self-awareness? Some schools are incorporating helpful and positive additions like peer support, and numerous other programs but they are limited in how much they can educate students about the mental and emotional aspects of life and the "self."

There are so many things that you can do and that are already being done to create positive and healthy change. If more of us were talking about it maybe it would become more commonplace to think about and act on new ways of relating to one another and to ourselves. Talking about it makes it less of an unknown. Let's talk about what is really going on with each other. Let children decide what is best for them and therefore learn (not forget) at a young age how to access Divine guidance. What parent doesn't want Divine help and support for their children and for their children to follow it. This is not "woo-woo" thinking, but Universal truth. Most have access to inner guidance. As parents, it is important to remember not to put your will onto your children but to recognize that they have their own inner guidance available to them. You can assist them by asking them to feel into what is right for them.

When you parent your children from the vantage point that they know what they need you can work together with them to problem solve from all perspectives. God doesn't command or punish but lovingly watches over us you while providing God's highest form of guidance and support. You are called to be with all of your fellow humans in this way as you navigate human life. Divine helpers help guide you in this way by blending together life experience, knowledge, education, personal style, personal circumstances and culture which is the foundation of each helper's offering of their gifts.

I recently learned a new phrase from the book "Pronoia," which is Deus Ex Machina. This term jumped out at me and I have been thinking about the ways in which this has interrupted my life and the life of those to whom I am close. The literal translation is God is machine. The definition that I understand is that God comes in and causes something sudden and unexpected to happen which changes the outcome of a situation and is usually the creation of a happy ending.

My mother is 85 and was having trouble walking and keeping her balance. She would get nervous that she would fall and wouldn't be able to call for help. She did fall a couple times which landed her in the hospital and then in skilled nursing to recover and get her strength back. She was very unhappy living in skilled nursing and afraid she would end up staying there indefinitely. My father had been moved there and never left until he passed away two years later. My parents had bought into a facility that had all three levels of care and my mother had been living independently until the falls. They weren't able to move her to the assisted living wing because it was at capacity and couldn't promise her when a room would become available. My mother was so unhappy in her current situation that I began looking for another place for her to live. Shortly after I began looking we learned that her brother and his wife would be moving from the east coast to assisted living nearer my home. My mother struggled most of her life with people and making friends but had always been comfortable with anyone who was family. Her parents had been from large families many of whom had moved to California. She didn't seem to feel judged with family in the way she did with anyone else. She was able to move into the same facility as her brother and his wife and now they take meals together three times a day. Many extended family members have already visited in the less than 6 months they have all lived together. It is convenient for everyone that they are all in the same place and she is receiving many more visitors than before when she lived further away. This is an example of Deus Ex Machina. She is more comfortable in assisted living than she ever was living independently and she has the company of family three meals a day and any other time she so desires.

I invite you to notice examples of Deus Ex Machina in your life.

The challenge is to find where the light gets in in spite of all the places that you may put up resistance. It is like the theory of squeezing something out. Instead of focusing on what isn't working, focus on what is and the more you focus on what is working, things begin to shift. Old beliefs and thought patterns that were stored in the unconscious, come into conscious awareness. If you notice any resistance you are being given the opportunity to use one of your self-healing tools to grow.

Ready to evolve?

Exercise: Get in touch with the part of you that is resisting – feeling negative, helpless, or hopeless and give

---

> *it unconditional love. Then sit in meditation and write down all of the beliefs that this part of you tells you. Notice where these beliefs are sabotaging what you would like to accomplish or achieve. Tell this part of you that he/she is not creating your life, you are. Give this part of yourself more love and let it know that you are in charge now. Thank it for helping you all this time but you are in charge now (Inspired by Ashley Lee).*

Continue to write as new awareness is brought to your attention. There is no right or wrong way to do this exercise as long as you are not resisting. Resisting can come in the form of continuing to think that how you are feeling is due to a person or a circumstance. The old language is to let go or think positively but as you shift your consciousness you are fine tuning the way you look at these things. The new language is to "Stand in Love, take Responsibility, see the Truth and find and create solutions inside of Love." The old thought systems were rooted in old programming that no longer serve. Our ancestors lived under different circumstances. The world is a much smaller place now that we travel by plane and we have the internet. This has opened up our ability to learn about different cultures, to learn about different religions, to learn about different lifestyles and lifestyle choices. Old programming was based on what people learned from their surrounding communities and leaders. We are moving away from thought patterns that tell us one person is better than another person, one way is better than another way. We now know that we do not have to live under the suppression of old programs. This is unprecedented in modern history. If what you think you believe and your thoughts are rooted in old programming, you may not know that change is possible (you can't teach an old dog new tricks). You can now change your thoughts and beliefs in ways we never knew we could. It seems so simple now but we have taken great strides for us to get here. The great masters knew this and tried to teach it to us, but it didn't seem attainable to ordinary people. The reason why this hierarchical system needs to be dismantled is because it disempowers people when the leaders or systems are of lower frequencies.

As a result of the industrial revolution, ordinary people could change the financial and social status of their families and a new term was coined "new money" vs. "old money." Once again, status was brought in, old money was of course more prestigious than someone who had had to work for their money. Then the trend shifted to criticizing those who were "born with a silver spoon in their mouth" to admiration for meritocracy, if you had worked your way up from nothing. That is when the tide shifted to applaud the hardest workers. At the same time that more opportunity came in, we lost sight of quality of life and became like machines. It became more and more difficult to attend to our spiritual needs. Our hearts were in the right places as we didn't want our children to endure the hardships that we had had to endure. We can change what we created by recognizing where we need to make changes. Each individual on their own individual path can discover how they were influenced by this suppression and change their thoughts. We no longer take for granted that whatever we thought before is "just the way things are." We can think whatever we want to create is possible and we now know that our thoughts are creating our lives.

Ready to evolve?

Exercise: Notice yourself trying to make sense of a feeling you are experiencing by looking around at your life and the people in your life to see what could be bothering you. Write down the feeling. People often mistake when they are feeling discomfort or discord that it must be because of people or circumstances. They feel anxiety and unconsciously and mistakenly think that something bad must be going to happen, or it is because they upset someone, or it is because they don't have what they want, or because they are a worrier or have self-judgments that they don't have it together or attribute how they are feeling to something not being right regarding work or at home. This feeling of discomfort or discord is the sign post pointing inwards and an opportunity to ask "What is it in me that is creating this

---

feeling?" Once you identify the feeling, ask yourself when in your life have you felt this way before? Think back as far as you can remember feeling this feeling. Write down 3 times in the past that you remember feeling this way.

Recognize that at some point in time in the past, there was a part of you that created a particular belief or set of beliefs that are the cause of what you are feeling in the present. Ask yourself whether or not the belief you created is true. Some common beliefs created in childhood are about worthiness, getting what we want and the belief that we deserve to be punished. Investigating the validity of the belief can help shift the belief to what IS true. Is it true that you are not worthy? Is it true that you deserve to be punished? Is It true that you are never going to get what you want and need?

After you have discovered your false beliefs, you can now replace them with what is true. If you don't quite believe it yet that they aren't true, then there are more beliefs to discover. When you have arrived at the place of knowing that what was created in the past is false and was based on a particular set of circumstances and what you knew at the time then you can create new truths.

I am worthy

I deserve love and understanding

I take responsibility for my thoughts and actions

I choose to be consciously aware of my thoughts and feelings knowing that I have the tools to change what needs to be changed

I empower myself through conscious awareness

I am sovereign

We have the ability to be the watchers of our awareness and we have the ability to draw from higher frequencies of energy when we recognize this.

CHAPTER 5

FULLFILLMENT

*The act or state of fulfilling: to
witness the fulfillment of a dream; to
achieve fulfillment of one's hopes.*

I s it possible to be fulfilled in every area of life? Most
people believe this a lofty ideal. How could it be possible
to construct your life such that you experience fulfillment in
every area? If you are fulfilling your life purpose you will
likely be fulfilled in every area of your life. If you are in
touch with your inner guidance this guidance will lead you
toward fulfillment in your everyday life in work, with your
family, in loving partnerships, and in your communities.
This way of living your life will transfer to Service to Us.
It is very different than striving for perfection in all ways.

Perfectionism is an addiction that many of us mistake for living a good life. People tend not to recognize that their efforts for fulfillment are thwarted when striving for perfection. As the universe weaves together the tapestry of your life, it brings it together piece by piece in a way that can only be done with the bigger picture in mind. It would be difficult to fathom exactly how to put together each and every facet since much of it we cannot physically see. All the inner and outer workings cannot be seen with the naked eye or necessarily always known with the linear mind. Much is revealed to us at the precise moment that it has been created and not a minute before.

There is a Chinese Proverb that goes something like this:

> *A farmer and his son had a beloved stallion who helped the family earn a living. One day, the horse ran away and their neighbors exclaimed, "Your horse ran away, what terrible luck!" The farmer replied, "maybe so, maybe not. We'll see". A few days later the horse returned home, leading a few wild mares back to the farm as well. The neighbors shouted out, "your horse has returned, and brought several horses home with him. What great luck!" The farmer replied, "Maybe so, maybe not. We'll see.*

Later that week, the son was trying to break one of the mares and she threw him to the ground, breaking his leg. The villagers cried, "Your son broke his leg, what terrible luck!" The farmer replied, "Maybe so, maybe not. We'll see."

A few weeks later, soldiers from the national army marched through town, recruiting all the able-bodied boys for the army. They did not take the farmer's son, still recovering from his injury. Friends shouted, "Your boy is spared, what tremendous luck!" To which the farmer replied, "Maybe so, maybe not. We'll see.

(Drmarlo.com)

It is not possible to understand situations in which all has not been revealed. As much as possible, if you can have faith and trust in the absence of proof you will alleviate the stress of perfectionism. We will alleviate much of the stress and anxiety in our modern society if we let this go. These are general terms and cannot cover absolutely every scenario but if enough of us subscribe to this thinking we will alleviate difficult and sometimes hopeless situations for everyone on the planet. Enough of us will be called and answer that call to help with everyone who is lacking basic needs. Everyone will have food, shelter, freedom and education. The universe has our back! We are connected in our oneness and will be helped and guided for the good of all. God doesn't leave anyone behind. We are all connected to the one channel of abundance and when we really recognize this everyone will benefit. There is enough for all.

The other question that comes to mind is "How do I know if I am fulfilled?" You may think you are fulfilled even when you are not. You may excuse doubts by telling yourself that you just need to practice gratitude because you obviously have everything it takes to be fulfilled. Gratitude definitely helps, but it is still important to discover if your lack of gratitude about your life is a message that you are not listening to your inner guidance. The angst you feel may be telling you that you are ignoring something vital that if acknowledged unlocks your next steps. The next steps are how you get from point A to point B, meaning from where you are to where you want to be in the fulfillment of your life's purpose.

My children have played video games for many years. Popular video games are designed much like life. Your character must complete quests to level up. Each quest is taken step by step and includes finding hidden items or secret places to unlock the next part of the journey. Your character doesn't know in advance what it will encounter in the journey which is sometimes dangerous or unexpected. Nevertheless, it is all a part of the design to get you to the next level. The design is continuously created as you take each step going to the right, going to the left. You are a co-creator making your contributions to the design of the tapestry with each step you take. You can create a life of fulfillment as much as you can create a life of suffering. You choose even if we are not aware of what you are choosing. Just like in a video game, each choice you make unlocks the next part of your journey and you don't always know what is around the corner but having trust and faith will help you to complete each quest along your journey without fear of the future.

Your worries about the future send you down a path that is based in fear. It doesn't mean that you don't prepare for retirement or that you should just go ahead and spend more money than you have, it means that if your decisions are fear based they may not be guided decisions. Since we are rooted in fear-based systems it is easy to do. We get caught up in the wave of the collective for fear of being left behind because we didn't do what everyone else was doing or what others suggested we do. There are general guidelines for living in this world but each situation is subject to particular details designed to get you to that next step. A person could be guided to make a decision that is counter to what would be advised but that in the long run will prove to be what was needed. Learning to listen to guidance and recognize it as such is a skill that is important to learn so that you know if the answer you are receiving is guided by your higher self or is based in fear.

It may take a little time to learn a way that works for you to receive information. It may work for you to listen to a feeling you get in your body, or to look in your mind's eye to see if your attention is directed upwards (yes) or downwards (no), or you can use self-testing or kinesiology testing to get yes and no answers. Over time, you will find what works for you. Whatever way you use it is important to combine it with what feels right to you and if an answer you receive doesn't feel right then it most likely needs more investigating. Combining your knowing with your test results will help you to fine-tune your skills. As children we came in with a natural sense of knowing but many of us lost this knowing during childhood as our experiences were invalidated or we were told how we were feeling was not the right way. Our abilities are still within but must be reignited after lying dormant.

Ready to evolve?
Exercise: Begin by thinking of a time when you just knew something and it turned out to be true. See if you can remember how you knew it. Did you "hear" it in your mind? Did you just know? Did you notice a lot of energy around something as you focused on it? Did you notice your energy drop as you focused on something as if to tell you that there was no energy there or that it was not true? Have you noticed when you were wanting to make a decision about somewhere to go that when you thought of all the choices there was one choice that just felt right even if you didn't know why? Practice focusing on your

heart center when you want to know something or want to make a decision. See what your heart is telling you via knowing, hearing, seeing in your mind's eye or sensing strong energy towards. You will learn that you can trust yourself and your inner guidance and have assistance that may not always make linear sense but turns out to be helpful.

You have everything you need to live a fulfilling life inside of you. Your thoughts and what you choose to focus on has a direct effect on the outcomes in your life. Bruce Lipton is one of the thought leaders who has brought what he learned in the laboratory to the mainstream. His scientific studies prove that cells change with focused thought. Thoughts projected on a cell will cause that cell to change form. According to Bruce Lipton's scientific research, our bodies are made up of cells that listen to and respond to our thoughts. Just as your cells respond to your focused intentions so do the circumstances and people in your life.

CHAPTER 6
FOCUS

*a central point, as of attraction,
attention, or activity.*

I would like to take a poll to find out how many people are living lives of fulfillment. In general, folks tend to focus on people and circumstances as being the reasons for why they are not fulfilled. There are major topics that are the usual suspects and are our "go to" for our issues. If your focus is that you don't have what you want then you will be shown more "not having what you want" otherwise known as "lack consciousness". According to experts and helpers who specialize in studying the law of attraction, this is how the universe works. So how do you handle working towards what you are guided to "want" without your focus being on what you don't have? You can direct your thoughts *to something like "I am working towards what I want and am guided to accomplish and am following each next step that I am guided to take". This is very different from focusing on working towards something you don't have and once you get there then you will be happy. Paying attention to how you talk to yourself is vital in creating the life you truly want. You may be thinking to yourself that you are doing the right thing and doing what you feel you are called to do and once you achieve what you are working towards you will be happy. You are not meant to postpone happiness and fulfillment. You are meant to experience it all along the way while you are "doing," whatever it is that you are doing. It is about the journey, not the destination.*

Sometimes you may go through something that is very painful and all you can think about is reaching the destination. The destination is to feel better. There are times where the pain is too unbearable to look in the mirror and remind yourself that you are "exactly where you are supposed to be." As difficult as those times may be, they are most often times of grief over loss and/or of shedding. You may be shedding old beliefs, old habits, thought patterns, what you thought you wanted, or things that you held on to and invested in. So many of us hold on to pain without realizing it and we continue to re-inflict pain on ourselves by holding on to what no longer serves us. We want someone else to come along and finally make it right but that day never seems to come and we continue to strive for that and put our focus and our energy on that even if we don't realize what we are doing. This usually brings us more pain, not to punish us, but so that we can see what we are doing. This gives us the opportunity to choose again. Part of what makes letting this go so painful is that we invested in the outcome looking a certain way and when we have to let go of this investment in time and in how it was supposed to look. Now that we know better we do better and as a part of the process might wonder what could have been. This feeling does pass as you grow in joy and fulfillment and see how what you went through helped you to learn to create the life you want instead of the life you had been creating that wasn't what you truly wanted or perhaps was only what you thought you wanted. You can take what you learn to help yourself and others so that they don't have to go down a hard path the way you did. When there is something in you or in your life that you do not want to face it is usually because you come from a place of fear that it will be too much to bear. You may have a belief that humans have to suffer. Hard work and suffering are the mainstay of progress. Running that program through our collective consciousness creates the need for people to suffer before change or progress can happen. We are shifting away from that program and that belief. We are beginning to learn about our oneness. We witness structures breaking down and mass murder continuing to be on the rise in our first world country. It is unfathomable that anyone goes hungry in our wealthy country or anywhere else in the world. As we grow in our abilities to listen to our inner guidance, spirit will make sure that we feed everyone and take care of all those in need. If everyone walks with spirit, spirit will lead the way. It doesn't matter what you call it "God," "Spirit," your "Higher self," "Love," "An instinct," a "Calling," or anything else but it does matter that you don't separate yourself from it.

You don't have to reinvent the wheel. Others have already done much heavy lifting so that we don't have to. We benefit not only from the efforts of those who have come before us, but also from those who are here now doing their calling. It may take one of these helpers several years or several months to work through a particular issue which helps to clear not only this issue from their life but at the same time is helping to lift this program from the collective. There are many helpers. We are all capable of being a helper in our own way and it starts with helping ourselves. We put on our oxygen masks first equipping ourselves with all that we need to forge ahead. It's not selfish to focus on yourself. You may need to lose weight, to clean out a cluttered room, to address anxiety or depression, to learn more about a particular subject that interests us, to face your husband or wife and address what isn't working in the marriage, to travel, to stop running away, to open your heart, to set boundaries with people who have crossed yours, to quit a job, to take a chance, to make an appointment with a therapist/healer, to start taking care of yourself in ways you know you need to, to stop taking care of everybody else at your own expense, to start caring more about others and less about your own fears, to find out what you are afraid of, to recognize that people and circumstances are not the cause, to stop blaming yourself, to have the courage to be grateful for where you are right now even if it's messy and not living up to the ideals you thought you held, to allow in joy, to meditate or connect with your higher self, to be kind to yourself in every moment.

> *"I lied and said I was busy; but not in the way most people understand. I was busy taking deeper breaths. I was busy silencing irrational thoughts. I was busy calming a racing heart. I was busy telling myself I am OK."*
>
> *Wild Woman Sisterhood*

As you heal, the world becomes a kinder place. You focus less on the perceived misdeeds of others and more on your own joy and your own passionate undertakings. You squeeze out what doesn't serve you in favor of that which brings joy.

The place you need to look for what you need to do is exactly where you are in your own life. You haven't failed and you are not behind. You have been creating and what you have created is already being used towards the fulfillment of your purpose. Now you can add to what you are creating. You add thought and action guided toward what you want to create and squeeze out what you don't want or what wasn't working in your life. Instead of focusing on what you can't do you can focus on what you can.

Ready to evolve?

Exercise: Put your hand over your heart and ask your heart what it wants you to know. Be with your question until you receive your answer. Do this every day.
  Inspired by Louise Hay

CHAPTER 7

WITNESS

*to see, hear, or know by personal
presence and perception.*

Y ou can bear witness to your own life and to your inner
workings.

Ready to evolve?

*Exercise: Write in your journal or notebook (You may want
to refer back to it later)*

What is the story you have been telling yourself for your entire life about your life? What are your beliefs about life?

About love?

About relationships?

About your worth?

About whether or not things work out for you?

About the world?

About people?

About religion?

About work?

About money?

About food?

About your body?

About God/Spirit/The Divine?

When you listen to your self-talk you learn what is in the unconscious. You may be making choices and creating things in your life that you don't necessarily want unbeknownst to your conscious self because of what is lodged in the unconscious. Your self-talk is revealing and is a gold mine if you listen to it. Many people say: Oh yes, I am definitely hard on myself, when I ask them if they have self-judgments. Folks think it is natural and normal to have self-judgments. "I am my own worst critic," is something to pay attention to. Your self-judgments are creating your relationships and your life circumstances. People can sense your unconscious beliefs even if you can't.

Are you on auto-pilot and telling yourself that you know what this life is all about? Have you trusted figures of authority to inform you about your spirituality, your education, your health and in trusting them forgot to ask yourself if it feels right to you? You are a co-creator. We need each other as we create together. We are moving away from giving ourselves over to someone or something who knows better. We are being guided to check with ourselves what feels right and what does not. We stand in our power and at the same time, honor the power of another. We honor every individual person knowing that only they know what their soul needs. We give respect for only they know what they have been through, only we know what we have experienced. We can't expect others to fully understand our journey. We must tend to our own emotions and feelings as we are the only one who truly knows what it is like to be us. We have become so good at hiding parts of ourselves from ourselves that we can't expect others to know what we do not even know about ourselves. We become our own best private detective discovering hidden mysteries in our psyche thus liberating ourselves from the jail cells we didn't know we created. The door was always open and the keys were always in our hand.

Ready to evolve?

Exercise:

This exercise is about the younger parts of yourself. Some people refer to it as an inner child or children. We can use this guided exercise to find the parts of our self that are still waiting, needing our attention. When we heal these parts of ourselves we become more conscious.

Choose a subject that is currently up for you meaning that it is something that is bothering you or something you are dealing with that is painful or uncomfortable, and you would like to be different.

Ask yourself if you remember having felt this "feeling" before. The circumstances may be different yet the feeling is familiar. And if you can, identify the feeling that you feel now that you have felt at some point in your past, preferably your childhood. You can do this exercise even if you have not yet identified the feeling.

Then ask yourself who is here?

How old is he or she? And do your best not to think but just let a number come to mind.

After you have the number, invite him or her to come and sit with you and imagine where you might sit. It could be your childhood bedroom, a beach, a park, a school, or anywhere you feel you and this part of yourself would be comfortable. Wait until you can picture in your mind's eye yourself sitting next to this young one.

Begin by letting this young one know that you are inviting him or her into your heart and you will never be apart ever again.

Notice how they are with you in the moment.

Are they comfortable or paying attention to you?

Are they looking away?

Do they leave and you need to invite them to come back?

Ask them what they need and wait. They may say something right away owr it may take them time.

If they don't say anything then you can begin by letting them know what you would like to say to them.

If you don't know what to say, imagine what you would say to a young child about that age. Would you tell them they are beautiful, smart, loved, capable, safe, perfect the way they are?

Let them know.

Notice how they react to what you are telling them.

Do they immediately want to give you a hug or do they just sit there and not react?

Some of them will take time to trust.

The important part is that you do not take your attention away or give up on them. They have been waiting a long time and it may take time for them to trust or believe that they will not be abandoned again or that they will truly get their needs met this time.

Ask them again what they need from you and wait.

If they tell you then give them what they need.

If they say, "I need to feel safe" let them know that they are in your heart now and you are taking care of them and you will never leave them again. You are sorry you left them and you will never leave them ever again. You didn't know you left them but now that you know you are going to take care of them from now on.

You are their mother now or their father now.

Even if you feel that you don't have it all figured out let them know that you may not have it all figured out but you will never leave them again.

Continue to ask them what they need from you and continue to give them what they need until they are done.

If they do not say anything just continue to reassure them that you will never leave them again.

If they say something that indicates they want to fix the situation as it was when you were young they may be still trying to take care of you. Let them know that they don't have to take care of you anymore or be strong anymore. They just get to be the young age they are and start growing up with you.

Show them around your home, introduce them to the people in your life (in your mind), let them know you are taking care of them now, this is where you live. Reassure them that you no longer live in the circumstances that caused them pain and they get to live the life that they want to live now. They have choice. Ask them what they would like to do when you are finished and leave them there doing what they want to do.

You can continue to check in with them and talk to them after the initial encounter if it feels right and again ask them what they need. It is common that people usually cry when doing this exercise. I have found that this exercise can be more powerful with a witness and recommend doing it with a trusted individual who can take you through it and ask you questions while you sit and relax.

I have found that the more difficulty an individual has been through the "stronger" they become. It is harder to break down barriers built by a strong person but worth it to go through to find the hidden gems waiting for them if they choose. These are subtle energies that are being addressed therefore in time things shift and one day you wake up and remember you used to feel a certain way and you haven't felt that way in a while or perhaps you notice that you just feel better. You still have your life that you had but you feel better. That is an indication of a profound shift even if people on the outside may or may not feel that your life looks profoundly different. The space opens for you to explore new territory in your life and in yourself. Relationships either improve or fall away in this process. Allowing yourself and therefore others to be themselves is key.

You don't owe anyone anything. I have been fortunate to have dear friends who are on their own journey of healing and self-discovery. I am grateful to have those with whom I can share what I am going through. We continue to learn from each other and from each other's growth. We consider a win for one of us as a win for all of us. Much of what we talk about is not linear and we appreciate having each other to talk about what we are going through. It is new territory for us and we know that if we weren't experiencing what we are experiencing first hand we would have a hard time understanding if another was telling us the same story. We are giving ourselves a chance to explore uncharted waters having no idea what the outcome will be. We are learning the meaning of having trust and faith in the absence of proof and are sometimes kicking and screaming. We have been strong and the walls are breaking down. It is helpful to have a friend who is also stepping out of their comfort zone. Sometimes you just need someone with whom you can have a reality check. Am I doing ok? Have I gotten off track? Is this real? As it doesn't follow linear guidelines it can be hard to find role models because our individual journeys may look very different. We are moving away from conforming with the norm therefore, in the beginning as we are learning to trust our inner guidance, may feel unsure about what we are doing. As we experience small wins we gain confidence little by little.

Once you reach this point you want to share. People often talk about what is going on in their lives and it is noticeable how different you will respond to what they are saying. You will no longer agree that they are not ok. You will no longer agree that the source of their problems are the people or situations about which they speak. It doesn't mean you don't listen with compassion but you are now a witness for everyone. You are a witness to the fact that they have everything they need inside of them to heal themselves physically, mentally, emotionally and spiritually. You no longer believe in suppression so you know that whatever their heart truly wants they can create. If they want more peace, they can have more peace. If they want less anxiety or less depression they can create that. You will no longer agree that they are a victim of their circumstances and will help them by being a witness to this. When you agree, you are projecting their story back onto them helping keep them stuck. Your projections hinder the receiver.

Your projections affect the people on which we place your projections. You are helping by not projecting the negative. You are helping by witnessing universal truth, positive reflections and miracles. Your thoughts are powerful in creating what you see and what you experience. Pay attention.

This is not the same as using your mental mind to repeat positive statements. You first need to see and experience them in yourself. You start with saying them and thinking them and allow yourself to work through what comes up in you such as doubt or disbelief to teach you what you need to learn. You can start by paying attention to when you project on others. You may notice a feeling of discomfort about not knowing what to do with the feeling that you used to project and while still believing that what you were projecting on another is true. You may experience growing pains but they don't have to be that intense or take very long to release. If you only knew how much help you really have you wouldn't be afraid, it is but for the asking. As it says in the bible, "Ask and you shall receive," the help is waiting. It was always there.

Johnny Cash wrote and performed music about being in prison in an effort to advocate for prison reform. He advocated to keep children out of prison and for rehabilitation. He used his connection with God and his voice for the greater good at a time when it wasn't popular to "care" about inmates. You wouldn't necessarily think of Johnny Cash's song about Folsom prison as "proof" without knowing about his efforts behind the scenes. He was ahead of his time.

The popular Starz series "Outlander" is a historical fiction. It is not only a love story but also a story that can help heal. It brings to light history between countries and is a small but helpful attempt to begin to heal the history of slavery in this country. It also sheds light on the history of love, treatment of women and hierarchical structures. We are far enough away from some of this history that we can see the harsh thinking that led to harsh treatment of gentle souls. The Holocaust Museum in Los Angeles is visual healing and helps us to not forget history to remind us not to make the same mistake. Creating the dark and negative also takes a step by step process and doesn't just happen overnight. When we stay aware of what process we are choosing we are not likely to make the same mistakes individually and collectively. Helpers use their gifts and talents to create various ways to speak to us.

I invite you to start looking for proof in your everyday life. You immediately change your perspective when you shift your focus to what is good in the world. You start by saying that you know the good is there. Then you "notice" in a way that you did not notice before because you have a new awareness that it is there. You just need to "see" it. You begin asking questions about what it looks like and the ways that it could possibly manifest. You might even think of ways that you can show it and be inspired to act upon any ideas you get to be the light at that time, in that place.

> *Lord make me an instrument of thy peace.*
> *Where there is hatred, let me sow love.*
> *Where there is injury, pardon;*
> *Where there is doubt, faith;*
> *Where there is despair, hope;*
> *Where there is darkness, light;*
> *And where there is sadness, joy.*
> *Oh, Divine Father, grant that I may not so much seek to be consoled as to console;*
> *To be understood, as to understand;*
> *To be loved, as to love;*
> *For it is in giving that we receive.*
> *It is in pardoning that we are pardoned.*
> *And it is in dying that we are born to eternal life.*
> 						*St. Francis of Assisi*

Sometimes you can just be in a place that inspires you to open your heart. Assisi in Italy was just that place for me. I took a trip in my early twenties with my brother around Italy for two weeks and we stayed a night in Assisi. We had lodging at a farmhouse style hotel and took a tour of the basilica complete with stories about St. Francis and about the people in the art inside the chapel, including Jesus. The tours are given by monks or brothers and ours was given by an American brother. By the end of the tour I was in tears. I felt a little self-conscious and walked outside to shake it off. I wasn't exactly sure what was happening but I knew that it was about love. Something had touched my heart deeply. That evening we had dinner at the farmhouse with the rest of the group. A young child sang for us and it was the most beautiful sound I had ever heard. My heart was truly still open and taking in all the love of the day. A Chinese man traveling with us told me that he could go home now, that he had come to Italy to find Christianity and after that experience he had found what he was looking for. In that moment I knew that I was not the only one who had experienced heart-opening love.

In the book, "The Tipping Point," Malcolm Gladwell describes different types of people that contribute to that point when something becomes popular. One of the types of people he describes he calls the "Maven," a person who knows a lot about one subject and is therefore a good person to ask for a referral or advice about that one particular subject. I believe that I am similar to this type of person as

I have been interested in and studying my entire life about psychology and healing and how to find happiness. This book can guide us to a tipping point for people to shift their focus to healing themselves and their communities. I have done my own personal research, tried out what works and what doesn't work on myself, and my clients and reached some conclusions. One conclusion I have reached is that there is a tremendous amount of help out there and that this help will appear if we ask. I invite everyone who is interested to not take my word for anything I have said but to go within and see if something or everything I have said resonates with you. Check it out for yourself, ask questions, read, talk to people, take classes, find your own way to embody God's mission for your life. Everyone has a purpose and everyone has guidance and help.

What would make someone want to step out of their comfort zone? Many people fear what they will find if they look inside and start digging. You may fear what you will find if you look and how it will disrupt your life. It doesn't cost anything if you change a belief. You may feel that you don't have the time or the energy to add one more thing to your to-do list or that if you are really honest with yourself about how you feel you will end up getting a divorce. You may feel that you would rather keep the status quo and the life you have. Perhaps you feel that your partner will not be amenable to problems or feelings or that you have already tried and it hasn't gotten you anywhere. You may fear the only option left is divorce. Many couples choose to suffer in silence after trying for many years and feeling that they were not able to reach resolutions. Individuals forgo working on themselves personally fearing they will have no choice but to leave their partner after facing the depth of their dissatisfaction. Miracles can happen when one partner goes within and uncovers what has been triggering them in the relationship. Relationships serve as mirrors to your unconscious. We often mistake getting frustrated or upset blaming the other for their actions or for something they said. If you instead notice that a strong feeling has been activated in you and ask yourself questions about what it is in you that is reacting in this way, you will be able to uncover and release the root cause to the trigger.

When one person in a couple stops participating in the destructive dynamic or exchange that they have previously been accustomed to, changes happen. Healing can take place when blaming stops. It is not just about fighting but also the subtle ways in which we sabotage our loving partnerships. When you stop agreeing with your partner that they are not "good enough" for example, you shift from being a part of the problem to a part of the solution. You become a witness seeing for them what they have previously not been able to see for themselves as a result of their childhood wounding. We need to hold each other up and at the same time what we are able to see in another, we are able to see in ourselves. You can only be a witness for what you know to be true within your own self. Therefore, taking your own personal journey can heal your relationship.

CHAPTER 8

PURPOSE

*The reason for which something
exists or is done, made, used, etc.*

"Maybe the journey isn't so much about
becoming anything. Maybe it's about un-
becoming everything that isn't really you, so
you can be who you were meant to be in the
first place."

Paolo Coelho

Your purpose is to be yourself via knowing yourself.
Your purpose is for Life to express Life through you.
Although this may look different in different lives we all
in essence want the same thing.

You already have everything you need inside your SELF. When you pick up a book and something resonates with you, it is you acknowledging that which is within you. When you listen to someone speaking about something that gets you excited and want to hear more, it is you recognizing that which is already within you.

It doesn't matter which author you choose to read or whether or not you choose to go to church, temple, synagogue or mosque. What matters is what resonates with you. What is speaking to you at this moment in time. What is speaking to you right now may change and something new may come that catches your attention. Follow it. Not in the way you follow a guru but, instead ask yourself what am I learning that is in me, from this? You may learn from that which bothers you about a belief that you have that is not true. You may learn from that which inspires you about the beauty that has always been with you. It's like the line from "The Wizard of Oz," "You always had the power my dear, you just had to learn it for yourself."

People can make suggestions about what might be of interest to you. They can point in the direction that might be helpful for you to look, but you have to look and see what is true and what is real for you. Only you know what your soul needs. Only you know how you are feeling in the dark of the night when you are alone. It doesn't matter if you are surrounded by people, you can feel alone when you are hiding from yourself. The difficult things that happen in the world are showing us that which we are hiding from our SELF. When we personally uncover what we are afraid to look at, we assist the collective SELF in uncovering that which WE have not seen about our SELF. If we only knew how impactful our contribution we would not hesitate to extend our selves. Each and every loving guided action taken, has a ripple effect throughout humanity.

When you begin with the knowledge that you have everything you need and make that your jumping off point, you can only go up. You are not broken, you are not beyond repair and you are not stuck being the way you are and cannot change and you are worth it. You are not too old or too poor, too set in your ways and it's not too late because the damage has been done. You are smart enough and you have what it takes. There is no goal to reach. The most important goal is to listen to your SELF and hear what it is telling you, to feel in your heart what you need to feel, and to act on your inner guidance. It is a beautiful thing when you begin to follow your guidance a little more each day. Things start to fall into place, what is not meant for you falls away, what is meant for you finds you and you learn to trust in the guidance that you are following because you keep having what feel like "wins."

You are not meant to suffer. That is an old program we have been running. Suffer also includes the belief in working hard/effort/force, giving up on your dreams for the sake of others, not believing that you have a purpose, thinking that you are selfish if you follow your heart, the belief that good things only happen to other people, and many other outdated beliefs. The quest for power brought in suffering at the deepest level. It also brought in oppression and hierarchy. All of this is beginning to unravel after thousands of years of living this way. It is unraveling because the highest expression of love in the world is growing at a rapid rate. We have reached a place of discomfort that is breaking our hearts open. We have been touched by fear and devastation causing us to re-evaluate our purpose. Due to technology, we get to know almost immediately events that are happening all over the world. We feel for people suffering from natural disasters, war, famine, government oppression, mass murder and injustices of all kinds.

Every day there is something in the news that makes us get in touch with the vulnerability of our human existence. History repeats itself and we no longer know where to turn. I am reminded of the woman who recently lost her son in the shooting in Thousand Oaks who was understandably distraught and stated that she "Doesn't want any more prayers, she wants gun control!" The definition of insanity is doing the same thing and expecting different results. Sending prayers after a shooting occurs hasn't stopped the next one from happening. It's not that prayers don't help because they do, it's that we also need to ask for answers for how to prevent this from happening in the first place. We need to ask and then we need to take guided action in order to get results. Part of our purpose is to take guided action when something is in our awareness. An action could be a specific action or it could be to recognize the consciousness for what it is. What was the consciousness of the person who did the shooting? Was it desperation? Was it mental illness? Was it hatred? Then ask ourselves, "When in my life have I experienced the feeling of desperation?" "When have I felt out of control mentally?" When have I felt the consciousness of hatred?" We can notice the consciousness that is being played out which is separate from the person. It is a consciousness. We don't forgive the horrific behavior. We forgive the consciousness which resulted in the behavior. Eventually, as we recognize and shine light on all expressions of consciousness, we will no longer express the lower states of consciousness.

We need less war-mongering and more strategies for waging peace. I have heard this said before and it seems reasonable to me, but I don't hear any stories about how we are doing this. If there are people in government working towards peace then let's talk about it. Let's focus on it and help it grow. We need to talk about all that is being done on behalf of gun control and peaceful solutions between cultures and countries and less on what we are against. Talking about what we are against doesn't help when we are judging the other side instead of understanding it. Let's talk about what we understand about what is happening. If we don't like the administration then let's talk about what we do like and how to get those folks elected. Let's spend more time focusing on what we are for than what we are against. This by no means, is a suggestion that we ignore when bad things happen. It means we notice when something is happening that doesn't feel right and we problem solve as to what we want and how to get there in a peaceful community forum. It is not enough if some of us are happy and a large percentage of us are not. Let's talk about how this came to be. Who isn't getting their needs met? How is it that our needs could be so different? Are they different? There almost wouldn't be a need for laws or at least no need to enforce them in this kind of environment.

It starts by imagining what is possible. We won't change a thing if we continue to tell ourselves this is just the way it is or that things don't change or any of the other rhetoric that keeps us doing the same thing. We are all in this together and it is impossible not to know that because we have all been touched by something on a global or community level.

If you follow your divine guidance, you would know what to do even if you aren't sure where each step you are guided to take will lead you. If you have trust and faith in your guidance, it will lead the way. You don't have to be an expert in everything, you can be guided expertly. It doesn't matter how spiritual you are or are not, if you know how to get in touch with something inside that gives you the sense about what to choose when you are making choices in your life, then you are already doing it. As you raise your awareness you will begin to notice that behind your guidance is a bigger purpose, in service to US.

This doesn't mean that we give all our money to charity

and work for free. You can do that if you choose or you are guided to but you may also be guided to procure great wealth and provide jobs and sustainable organizations that are for the good of many. You may be guided to share the wealth and provide your employees with share- holders benefits instead of keeping the wealth in the hands of the few. Consciousness supports businesses too. Just like consciousness fuels every cell, atom and molecule in your physical body, consciousness is also in every endeavor you undertake either helping you to learn or showing you Love's expression of love through your business. You are always utilizing life force energy either to contract or to expand and sending that out into the collective atmosphere. When you are in survival mode you are in contraction. Some circumstances of survival cannot be avoided, while others are a result of our unconscious programming from the past.

Many of us had this program passed down to us by our ancestors who went through World Wars I and II and The Great Depression, Viet Nam and the Korean wars. You may think that you are not affected by something that happened 80 or 100 years ago but you can be. We still need to heal the effects of slavery and the occupation of this country and how Native Americans were treated. We are being shown that this is still being passed down from ancestors. Individuals need healing due to what they inherited that didn't get completed in the lives of their ancestors. When a life is ended and resolution is not completed, those who come after you will bear the burden of needs that were not met and that went unresolved. Families of slave owners were often victims of abuse as well. No man who could do what was done to slaves, was capable of love or kindness in his own life or family. The fracture in society at that time was severe. There is no possible way that love could have even been remotely present and those actions could still have been taken. No way possible. The families suffered in different ways but, nevertheless, they also suffered. They lived in forced silence. They were in no way living in torture the way the slaves were but what they did endure was passed down from them to future generations. They passed down disempowerment that also needs to be healed. They passed down emotional disconnection that still exists as a result of what happened 200 years ago. They passed down a disconnection from love, the true sense of the meaning of love that we are still dealing with to this day.

Part of our purpose is to heal the past in the present moment. It is not necessary that you know specifically what happened to create the consciousnesses that are being expressed in your family; but more important to know what consciousness it is so that you can change it, heal it and grow from it.

You are either contracting or expanding.

CHAPTER 9

AGAPE

Love

L *ove has many definitions. The definition of love that I am referring to in this chapter is called the "agape" kind of love. What is agape love and how is it different from other kinds of love? "Agape love means action. It means we act in a loving way towards others." Posted on February 12, 2015 by Christine Crosby in "What's Hot."*

What I am suggesting is you act in a loving way towards others and towards yourself at the same time. What is good for "others" is good for you. It does not mean giving your power away for the sake of others or making yourself uncomfortable so that others can be comfortable. It means following your inner guidance which can often guide you to do what feels right for you even if others don't agree.

Why is it important that you lead with love? Why do you not just continue on the road you have been traveling? Our children are going to school, graduating and getting jobs. We are taking better care of ourselves. You can get healthy meals delivered for a relatively affordable price so that you don't have to interrupt your busy lives to plan, shop and prepare. Most of us have more financial resources than our parents did. We travel all over the world. We are able to educate ourselves about most subjects thanks to the internet in a moment's notice.

So why focus on the subject of love? Aren't you doing the best you can in your own life and that is the best you can hope for? What does that even mean "Service to us"? Aren't we in service to us by taking care of ourselves so that we are not homeless or in jail and thus draining society's resources for our care? There really isn't time for much else after we go to work and school, exercise, eat right, go to church or do whatever we do to take care of our spiritual needs, take care of our relationships and anything else we are involved in, is there? We are already doing the best we can with what we've got. You may be involved in a divorce or dealing with a child who has lost his/her way. You may have a health issue that is taking all of our time and energy to deal with. You may be dealing with a financial crisis or trying to keep a business afloat. There are many issues that you may find yourself having to face.

Love is present regardless of what you are doing or what you are dealing with. It is standing at the door beckoning you to follow it. It is offering its love and guidance, its support and help in every circumstance and in every relationship. "What would love do?" is the question you can ask yourself in every situation. We complicate what we are working on with fear of the unknown. We can ask this question in politics. How would love allocate available resources? Would love send troops outside of the country and if so, what would love have them do? It really is that simple. Why are we using love as a guidance system?

When you ask the question, "What would love do?", while standing in love, what would you determine needs to be done to change a situation or circumstance? It is important to have understanding about how you got here so you can see that this isn't just how it is and cannot be changed. How you change things lives solely in the present. If you harbor resentments about the past and allow them to get in the way, they will. What you "will" has an effect on what you do. If you "will" that are a victim and are not willing to move into solution then you will continue to feel a victim and continue to give energy to perpetrator consciousness. Love is always present but doesn't create the feeling of victim. Love doesn't create the feeling of being the oppressor either. Love doesn't create the kind of power that is born of force. Love creates in "power" not "force." Love takes action. We have freedom of choice. "Love" is the answer to all situations.

Love and Joy abound residing in the same house always. If it costs making yourself vulnerable is that a price you are willing to pay for joy? If it costs looking at what isn't working in your life, is that a price you are willing to pay for joy? If it costs learning to listen to the voice inside you in the stillness is that a price you are willing to pay for joy? If the reward is that you are assisting the world in becoming a better place for the children and grandchildren, is that a benefit you are willing to take action for? What are you willing to face on the road to joy? Are you willing to face yourself? Are you willing to face outdated beliefs, fears about change, the possibility of losing the identity that you built for yourself so that you can discover the truth about who you really are? Are you willing to risk discovering that the purpose you thought you were working toward may not be what you thought? What if you get to keep the life you have but be happy even though you thought that may not be possible, would you choose that?

You may fear the outcome will be the worst possible outcome so then you don't lean in. What part of you is fearing the worst? It is usually the part of you that has untrue beliefs about life and about love that tells you it won't happen for you, can't happen for you and now you shook things up in your life and made things worse. For example, I have a friend who quit her corporate job after 30 years to follow her dreams. After quitting her job, it wasn't exactly clear where her path was going to lead. At first, she was trusting and proud of herself for choosing what felt right to her rather than holding on to what she knew. A few years in, she was guided to heal the past in preparation for what was coming. Through her healing journey she met new people and her path began to unfold without having to make an effort. She is now taking inspired action and creating her new vocation that includes incorporating what she learned in her previous career. Her new work is in Service to Us and she is leading others to do the same.

Ready to evolve?

Exercise:

Lovingly speak to the ego part of yourself that is at times in charge of creating your life and let them know that you are in charge of creating your life now. Give them unconditional love and let them know that they are benched. You are the one who is going to be in the game and they can watch from the bench. You are not sending them away, you are inviting them to watch from the sidelines as you create your life.

Now you can go out and create your life the way you want to create it. You can dream it into being. It is no mistake that you have the life you have because you created it. There are opportunities in everything. Opportunities to love, to find meaning in all that you do, and to help all of humanity through each loving guided action. Something as seemingly small and simple as putting your hand on your heart and asking yourself "What do you want me to know today?" falls into the category of helping humanity. Can you imagine if everyone did that every morning, received a guided action and then followed it? Trusted it even if they didn't exactly know what it meant or where it was taking them? Life on earth would have the opportunity to become the most well-orchestrated, life-affirming, loving beyond limits symphony making the most beautiful music out of all of our resources on earth.

We are dreaming this now or I would not be writing this. Imagine how impossible it appeared that humans would fly in the sky like birds and now it is one of the most common forms of transportation with thousands of flights each and every day. What you focus on serves as a prayer for what you want to create. If everyone joined in a collective vision it would be much easier to create this beautiful world we know in our hearts is meant for US. In the quiet space when we are not activated or in fear, we know the truth of our essence, the truth of our being-ness. What miracles are possible without a powerful force in the universe? How do we explain the miracles, the mystery?

SHARON TAWFILIS M.A.

If you have the freedom to create whatever you want and the only thing it costs you is that you change your belief, would you want to choose that? What is it that makes people cling to what they think they know? They choose the dishwasher behind door number one because they think they are going to end up with the donkey and would rather play it safe than risk everything for the trip around the world! You get to have the life you have now and take all that you have learned and bring it with you in Service to Us. All of your experiences and the knowledge you have gained are used in service to the expression of what inspires you and in commitment of your purpose. The Divine is practical in the way that nothing goes to waste. All of your experiences provide you with the knowledge to assist you in offering your gifts. Once you step into your passion everything you need to know has already been put in place. Your rich life experiences build bridges to relate to others even if what you are doing now is very different from the way you lived your life in the past.

As you grow in your intuitive practices, you can receive messages as to why you are being guided in certain directions and to do certain things. Many things take time and dedication to unfold therefore having some ideas about the possibilities will help provide you with direction and the motivation to stay the course. It still requires "faith and trust in the absence of proof" to believe that you are being guided for a reason even though it doesn't look like what you are working towards is likely to come to fruition.

92

Faith and trust are essential when the proof has not yet materialized in the physical world. There are countless examples in history whereby people thought someone was crazy who was working diligently on a project and never giving up while life was busily going on around them and people were seemingly making progress while they appeared to be standing still. Then suddenly the time was ripe for the unveiling of the new invention or the new way of being and everyone who laughed or didn't believe now sees. Your circumstances may or may not be quite so dramatic to the outside world, but may feel like a huge leap of faith compared to what you are used to. When you choose to open to the unknown, a space opens up so the new can come in. The Divine can guide and assist you, but it is up to you to see the opportunity in everything. You may choose to stay stuck in old patterns or old beliefs when things happen or go into victim mode or get triggered. You may choose thoughts such as "Things don't work out for me," or "I don't get what I want."

If you are in the practice of consulting your intuition you are less likely to go into a downward spiral. You will be able to understand better why certain things are playing out such as they are. It doesn't mean that you don't experience emotions, or grief or regret as things shift or change, it just means that you will have some understanding that the changes are not just random. It doesn't mean you won't grieve the loss of a marriage if you are guided to divorce. It doesn't mean that you will agree with every step along the way but eventually you will see the wisdom in everything and find that you get to be happy. You get to live a fulfilling life.

It is important to find joy in moments along the way. You are guided along the way with twists and turns and there is the opportunity for joy and fulfillment at each step. It is only you who stand in the way and say you will be happy "when" you reach your goal. There really is no "there". We offer our services in service to "US" and are woven into the fabric of life with each and every choice that is made by you and by others. A situation may be created by others and we find ourselves called to step in to help. It is important that we pace ourselves and that we honor our own down time and the Divine will honor it too. We are not guided to exhaust ourselves in service. We are guided to put on our oxygen mask first and take the best possible care of ourselves so that we have what it takes to follow our guidance. We need to heal, we need to find out why we have anxiety and address the root of that, we need to attend to all the things that would cause us to have low energy and be pursuing what inspires us at the same time. Both are equally as important. Outside of extreme circumstances, it is more important that you have balance than rush into "completing" your calling. You have purpose, you are important and you are loved no matter where you are in the process of your life path. If you ignore your calling you will most likely get more and more uncomfortable or dissatisfied with your life circumstances or you may get a health issue to get your attention. It is just the Divine tapping you on the shoulder and letting you know that there is something for you to pay attention to.

There are many teachers who have spoken about this concept. I am not reinventing the wheel. I am guided to gather information and put it in such a way that some will be reached who perhaps would not have been reached. Some folks have other callings and have been focusing in other areas so that they can bring their gifts to the world. Perhaps it is for them that I have gathered information that I can pass along. And yet, for others it may be that they discover they are not alone in their interests and receive confirmation that there are many of us out there wanting to change the focus of humanity's existence to a life affirming expression of Love that has never been seen before.

Just when you think you know, things change, which is why you often are guided to give up strong beliefs you have carried with you, often for generations. Giving up beliefs that gave you energy and hope to keep going can be a daunting undertaking if you are not ready. We continue to evolve as a species and therefore while we were required to focus on survival for eons we have now moved into a new age. There are many people on the planet who are still living in circumstances that allow them to barely be able to feed themselves. Given the fact that most of the world has reached a different level should give us pause. This great divide should be a sign for us that we are not paying attention to a part of our "Self." We can change that belief to the knowing that there is enough food and resources for every human being to live a fulfilled life. When you change your own beliefs about your own life and create fulfillment and abundance, you are contributing to the changing of our collective beliefs that will relieve the suffering of others on the planet. It is not always easy to connect the dots as to how your seemingly small changes contribute to huge changes on the planet but imagine if enough of us changed this belief that we have as a collective. We would end world hunger.

I recently saw a video clip on CBS Sunday morning featuring a man explaining that he decided to find one thing he is grateful for then follow the trail of gratitude and thank every person along the way. He chose to express gratitude for his daily cup of coffee. He expressed awe and surprise how many folks he ended up thanking for his cup of coffee from the delivery truck drivers to the people who pave streets and make paint for the yellow lines that keep us safe. He also included such people as the ones who keep bugs out of the coffee in the warehouses in the country where the coffee is grown. This was a fine example of how we are all interconnected and truly need each other on this journey. When we attend to the needs of all of "US" we will end world hunger, mass shootings, war and disease. Each of us has a part in this and all are called. There is nothing to feel ashamed or guilty for there is only our calling to answer. When we know better we do better.

CHAPTER 10

CHANGE

to make the form, nature, content, future course, etc. of (something) different from what it is or from what it would be if left alone.

*I*s there something in your life that you are afraid to change? Is there something that you fear you would have to give up if you were to address the things in your life that are asking for your attention?

You may fear change and what it will require that you let go of. As a result of this fear of the unknown, you create blocks to your ability to open to all the abundance that the Divine is waiting to bring into your life if you give up the illusion of control. You get to have the life you have but be happier. If you willingly want to make changes then you will be supported in that. We get confused and may judge ourselves thinking that we are ungrateful for what we have if we feel a sense of unease and find ourselves wanting "more." It is usually not that we are not appreciative of what we have, but that we have reached a place in our lives that we can move into the service of our calling if we are not already fully in it.

I have had clients who have had successful careers and done very well for themselves financially who are feeling the "heat" of wanting more. Some become depressed and go into story. They tell themselves the story that they have wasted their lives doing something that has been lucrative and provided for their families but hasn't given them the feeling that they are serving a higher purpose or calling. They may feel that it is too late or that they cannot possibly leave what they are doing to pursue something as yet unknown. They are not in touch with what it is that they are being called for or at least they feel they have no idea where to look. They often feel guilty for "wanting" more as they have had so much success as defined by the collective version of success. It is common that folks experiencing something like this are afraid they have wasted their time but in truth they will be called to bring all of the skills and talents they have acquired in their lifetime doing exactly what it was that they were doing that they deemed "not my purpose."

The universe does have a plan for all of us and all of us are called. A new time has arrived where we are *being called to fulfill our potential and are being helped in our efforts to do this. Up until now, so many of us have not chosen to answer our calling. There have been enough helpers who have forged their way in spite of the lack of support they may have received from family members or from the pressure of fitting in to a societal norm. These helpers have broken through these norms without having to actually leave their communities. They have found a way to merge both following their calling and fitting in with society. They get to keep the lives they have and they get to fulfill their purpose. These helpers have paved the way for this new way of viewing life and success, love and relationships. A tipping point is emerging where it will be popular to talk about such things.*

If you have trust and faith, it will assist you in the transition to this new way of approaching your life and in teaching your children. Already there is talk about how to structure our education systems to better serve each individual child. One idea is that children will only take courses that they have shown an interest in or aptitude for and will not be required to learn subjects in which they have no interest. This would assist all of us in fostering our potential from a young age. Imagine a world where we look to see what each individual child is geared towards and then foster those subjects. We would be assisting the process of opening up to our individual callings from an early age. If each of us were to receive assistance in fostering what we are being guided to do there would be less anxiety and less depression, less failed marriages and more of us living fulfilling and productive lives. If all of us lived our lives guided in Service to US, we will all live happy productive lives. We will all be fortunate and the environment will be cared for and will include all people in all countries.

We are being guided into unprecedented times: times of peace, times of joy, times of seeing the Divine in each and every one of us. We truly are all one and loved by God. It seems so simple when it is stated in such a way. We have complicated things out of our belief that we are separate from God, that we are separate from one another.

If I am writing this, there are many dreaming this into existence. Simply by stating that it is possible can make it so. We may experience growing pains but we do not have to. It doesn't have to be painful to open our minds. We are not required to rush into things that do not yet feel comfortable. We are merely being asked to open our minds and our hearts to see the possibilities and to see new ways. It is our unconscious wounds that make it difficult to let go of old beliefs. When we release those, things become more clear. We can stay right where we are, but see things anew. We can live in our houses, go to our jobs, take care of our children, go on our trips, get married, get divorced, take care of our elders, go to church to worship, follow our creative and artistic calling, make movies, write books, run our governments, educate our youth, care for our environment, run our businesses and just about anything else we can think of AND ask ourselves what else may be meant for us.

If you are open to change, then you give license for pronoia to bring you magic. When you allow change to come into your life, new doors open.

All of us are called to make our own unique contribution to the planet. You are here to be the embodiment of God's love. You are here to be the physical expression of the Divine and you are here to love. Most of us do not realize that we don't know the true meaning of love. We mistake want for love. We mistake need for love. We mistake fear for love. When we make mistakes in our interpretation of what love is we make mistakes in other places as well. This is how we complicate things. When you begin to unravel what is true from what is not true things seem much less complicated. All of life becomes more and more clear. When you feel clear, there is less fear and more love. Unconditional love is the only love that is real. Unconditional love can feel threatening to those who cling to their conditions. We cling to conditions out of fear that is created from the beliefs we still hold in our conscious and unconscious. When you clear the unconscious, it becomes easier to make conscious choice. It becomes easier to stand in love.

When you stand in love, you find love for yourself. You may find love for the life that you have regardless of whether or not your circumstances have changed knowing that you get to have what you want. You find the love that guides you to change what you need to change so that you can live the fulfilled life we are ALL meant to live. One of us finding fulfillment will assist others in finding theirs. We are all interwoven into this fabric of life and what assists one of us in finding peace and fulfillment will be interwoven into the fabric of a collective peace and fulfillment. More than just one of us will be helped. One of us finding love, peace, wealth, fulfillment and good health is a win for all of us. With this new way of thinking we will celebrate more and more the achievements of others knowing that these achievements are the good news that we are all headed towards for ourselves. We will lift each other up even if it hasn't been your "turn" yet. You will celebrate knowing that each time someone succeeds you are that much closer to your own individual success. Helping others succeed will be a part of your purpose. You will feel rewarded by lending a hand in service to our purpose, in Service to Us.

We will live lives of interdependence as opposed to independent and codependent. We can have all the values of living interdependent and still keep our individual homes and possessions. If business owners and corporations are operating in Service to Us, they will still be the owners but will be more inclined to share the wealth for the greater good. It doesn't mean that we all have to have equal distribution for everything to be fair but no one will ever have to go without. Our priorities will change and we will be compensated with fair wages for sustainable lifestyles. To some, this may sound threatening and to others a breath of fresh air and a long time coming. No one need feel threatened when all are taken care of and all are living fulfilling lives doing what it is they were meant to do. Just because we lost our way doesn't mean we can't answer our calling to get in touch with it. We can switch tracks to a sustainable future, one step and one person at a time. There is no place that we will arrive as we only have what is right now in front of us. We can dream into being a world where everyone belongs, experiences peace and fulfillment, and has everything they need. If you wonder how you can possibly change the world you may feel overwhelmed at the thought of taking on such a feat single-handedly and want to quit before even starting. However, someone, who wants to live a life of purpose and fulfillment is more likely to feel inspired to take action for the sake of living a happy life. You will think globally and act "locally."

It doesn't cost anything to change your beliefs. It can be as simple as changing an outdated belief that makes the difference between living a life of fulfillment and therefore "happiness" or a life of status quo. You may want certainty and predictability and you can have a measure of this but it may not be in the way you think. If you allow yourself to be guided and work through any resistance you feel about what presents itself, you will see the divinely woven fabric come to life before your eyes. You will learn to understand and to appreciate what is brought to you. You will see that there is much more than meets the eye. People aren't always what they seem and the things you may have once thought important may turn out to be not all that important after all. As you bring into your awareness how things came to be you may see them differently than what you thought was truth or what you thought was fact wasn't that at all.

Ready to evolve?

Exercise: Sit in solitude and ask yourself what your heart wants.

This is one way to find out what is meant for you. The further away you are from being in touch with this, the more there may be to uncover. It may start with something on the surface level until you are able to get to the real pearl underneath it all. One of the most common reactions people have is to fear losing what they have. They immediately jump to, "Well, I can't leave my job because people are depending on me." "I can't talk to my husband about how I feel because he will just get angry and I would rather not say anything and keep what I have than rock the boat" is another common fear reaction. This immediately shuts down the possibility of finding what your guidance wants you to know before you even have the chance of learning that it isn't what you fear. If you feel your guidance is leading you to a life of peace and fulfillment and you feel that couldn't possibly happen while you work in this job or stay in this marriage then you have missed a step.

You can say, "Ok God, if I am being Divinely guided to a life of peace and fulfillment and I don't see how I could ever have that in my current circumstances then show me." Ask God to show you how to get there. Fear will undoubtedly come to the surface accompanied by all those old false beliefs that you can't have what you want. These beliefs may sound like, "I am not good enough" or "Who do you think you are that you could have it all", in an effort to shut that down right away. Your ancestors may have passed that belief down to you having lived in much different times. With all the help that we have and with all that we now know, we don't have to carry those limiting beliefs any longer. Many of us have already broken through some of the stories that were passed down to us. Part of the reason they continue to get passed down is that we don't question "The way things are," and just take for granted that that is the way it is. We don't ask how certain beliefs were created and if it is right for us to continue believing what was taught. If we teach our children that we know what is better for them than they know for themselves we are doing them a great disservice. We can teach them our values while allowing them to discover for themselves if what we value is what is right for them. We can teach them to be empowered and that they have choice and allow them to make their own decisions. If we are able to openly communicate with one another they will feel free to discuss their choices and we can help them in more practical ways. We may have discussions about what they want to create and what they feel they want. It is important that we keep ourselves in check and not try to persuade them in one way or another in an effort to truly let them choose even if it is not what you would want them to choose. If, for example, your child comes to you and tells you that they just want to surf all the time and that they are not really interested in working except to be able to pay rent you may have to bite your tongue but you can walk them through what that looks like. Your child may even go all the way through choosing what you would not wish for them to choose and then living their choice and deciding that they do not wish to live that way. It will have been their choice. They may also be following their own guidance that if they had not felt free to follow may have derailed them finding their true calling. Their true calling could be something that comes from following what they want to do and finding a business they want to start that could have only come from living with 5 people in a cramped apartment by the beach. If we have faith and trust in the absence of proof we will be guided to what is our true and highest good and we are not meant to struggle.

When you accept that only your soul knows what you need, you usher in a deeper form of acceptance, an "allowing." When you allow for everyone's individual expression of themselves you make room for guidance. You become a witness to the evolution of consciousness in each of us.

CHAPTER 11

ALLOWING

To give permission to or for; permit.

A *deeper "allowing" ushers in a new consciousness. We are sensitive beings that, due to difficulty or trauma, shut down parts of ourselves in order to survive the harshness of our circumstances or the harshness of the actions of those around us. What people don't realize is that in doing so you have shut down your real strength. We have disconnected ourselves from our true spiritual connection. We did this out of fear thinking that it was our best chance at survival. Then, we built structures around this way of surviving to protect what we have created. We continued to strive, taking us further and further away from who we truly are. We lost sight of how the earth was designed to sustain us, providing us with plant medicine, plenty of food and water, as well as materials for providing ourselves with shelter. It is time to press the reset button and remember who we really are.*

When you unravel the ways in which you have blocked yourself from being in touch with your true nature and with nature itself you may find it easier to access the Divine. Part of the problem is that we don't know what we don't know. We don't know that we don't love ourselves.

We don't know that in our wanting the best for ourselves and for others that we still aren't in touch with the truth of who we are. We don't recognize that when we get triggered it is not the circumstances or the people around us. We expend energy trying to "fix" these things and correct the actions of others to suit our comfort levels instead of uncovering the beliefs in our unconscious that led us to activate the energy of fear. We spend inordinate amounts of time in fight or flight every time something triggers us. When you "feel" something, if you allow yourself to feel whatever it is that you are feeling, instead of jumping into action in an effort to make it go away, you will assist yourself in this unraveling.

Allowing gives the feeling of anxiety the opportunity to teach you the next thing you need to learn ony our quest to know thyself.

Anxiety is an epidemic that we don't talk about in that way. We talk about the medications that will help calm the anxiety. We talk about all the ways in which we are working to perfect all the areas of our lives but we don't talk about the anxiety that is the result of the focus of perfection. We focus on all of life's imperfections in ways that convince ourselves that if each of these items would correct itself we would be able to feel less anxiety. We don't allow ourselves to just "be." In our effort to keep up the structures we have created and our place in them, we strive to keep things the same even if there is a voice inside of us that is pointing to change. The corporate CEO that has been depressed for 20 years because he hasn't been listening to this voice of change, to the stay at home mom who feels trapped but blames it on an unhappy marriage, the young person new in his career not understanding how he could be having a premature mid-life crisis are all examples of folks who are not listening to what is natural and inherent in them. The CEO keeping the door slammed shut on looking into what he is feeling fearing that he will only realize that he hates his job when the truth may be that he is being guided to stay in his job but create change from within that structure. The stay at home mom whose husband is an alcoholic can't see her part in what they have created together and fears that she will struggle on her own but if she would look inside herself may find that she could bring healing to her entire family and find love once again for the man she never thought could redeem himself in her eyes.

We trust what looks good on the outside even if we are struggling on the inside. We would rather be living a life that looks good to others than a life that feels good to us. We think that what looks good on the outside feels good and tell ourselves that we are being ungrateful if it does not. It is difficult to speak in generalities as not everyone is dealing with the same issues. All are called in different ways, but there is an epidemic of keeping up with things. You may want to keep up what looks good to your family and what is expected of you, or you may be trying to keep up with what looks good in society but you will not be able to be happy or fulfilled if you are not listening to yourself first and foremost. There are many of us now who are listening to that still small voice inside making it safer for all of us to follow suit. It may not seem like such a courageous feat to listen to yourself but if we are honest we have many fears that we will have to let go of things we think we can't let go of.

So many of the inspiring stories we read about from people who changed their lives for the better, tell about things that were let go. In the book "Eat, Pray, Love" Elizabeth Gilbert allowed herself to let go of all that had been expected of her regarding marriage. In the book, "Wild," about the woman who went to find herself on the Pacific Coast Trail, she let go of all creature comforts to find that still small voice inside. Eckhart Tolle became homeless on a park bench leaving a professional teaching position not knowing that he would teach again but in a new way. Not everyone will be called to take what may seem like drastic measures. Society would be in chaos if we all suddenly stopped what we are doing. We can however, begin by learning to LISTEN and then ALLOW what is calling us to come in and teach us on this wild and wonderful journey.

"The Summer Day" by Mary Oliver

Who made the world?
Who made the swan, and the black bear?
Who made the grasshopper?
This grasshopper, I mean—
The one who has flung herself out of the grass,
The one who is eating sugar out of my hand,
Who is moving her jaws back and forth
*   instead of up and down –*
Who is gazing around with her enormous
*   and complicated eyes.*
Now she lifts her pale forearms and
*   thoroughly washes her face.*
Now she snaps her wings open, and
*   floats away.*
I don't know exactly what prayer is.
I do know how to pay attention, how to
*   fall down*
Into the grass, how to kneel in the grass,
How to be idle and blessed, how to stroll
*   through the fields*
Which is what I have been doing all day.
Tell me, what else should I have done?
Doesn't everything die at last, and too soon?
Tell me, what is it you plan to do
With your one wild and precious life?

We would automatically usher in the energy of allowing if we honored each other by asking what they are guided to do and support them in doing it. We would also get to witness the unfolding of the beauty of the lives of those close to us. And, naturally, we will see new things happening in our communities. It might be a slow burn, but the shifts will be lasting. Most of us do not want radical and drastic change. We may say we do when discussing such topics as politics or climate change, but in our own personal lives most of us are not willing to do what it takes to assist the process that would allow for radical and drastic change. When you shift from fear to love it is done in that very moment even if nothing has changed on the outside. Addressing what it is in you that is seemingly preventing you from shifting to love will help.

Love is your natural state when you allow it to come in. Love guides you, love takes care of you and love provides for you. Love works out problems. Love is organized and efficient. Love utilizes what we have to work with and nothing goes to waste. Love is kind to others. Love takes care of the earth, which is perfectly designed to take care of us. Love runs governments and schools. Love has a solution to every problem under the sun. Love isn't only something you do when a newborn baby is born or when you attend a wedding but you set it aside when it is time to go to war. Love is not something you set aside when you go to your corporate job because you are being told that the only thing that matters is the bottom line and not the people working for you. Love is not something to be set aside in competitive sports because the object of the game is to win. What we focus on is what we are Willing. If you focus on what you don't have you are willing to not have. If you focus on everything you are grateful for you are Willing for more to come in. If you focus on the reason that you are focusing on not having, you will find the reason so that you can release it in order to shift to Love. Ask and it is given to us.

There is a book by this title and a quote in the bible that states, "Ask and you shall receive." Ask why you are not feeling fulfilled in an area of your life and you will be guided to the answer so that you can bring every area of your life to a state of health. This is not the same as trying to make your life perfect. Trying to make your life perfect is rooted in looking at what you don't have and trying to force it. Our world is, in many ways, upside down. What we think is important we eventually find out wasn't what we thought. Until we make peace with decisions and choices made in the past and understand what it was we thought when we made those decisions and choices, we will feel regret. When we begin awakening we realize we are not the same person we used to be. Our life may look much the same on the outside, but we may feel very different on the inside. We don't have to do anything at all that we do not want to do. We don't have to shift. We don't have to change. We don't have to listen to our guidance or follow our calling. We have freedom of choice.

> *"We shall not cease from exploration, and at the end of all our exploring, will be to arrive where we started, and know the place for the first time."*
>
> *T.S. Eliot*

CHAPTER 12

CONSCIOUS

Aware of one's own existence, sensations, thoughts, surroundings, etc.

*W*e are being shown that we are all expressions of the Divine and using Divine power to create our lives. *You have the power to create what you want. You have the power to create. You are creating. You are powerful. Do you want to create by default or in conscious choice? Do you want to be conscious as you create so that you know what it is that you are creating? Being nice and having good intentions does not constitute creating in consciousness. There is so much more involved than just the feeling that you want something good for yourself and for others. All you have to do is look in your life for what jumps out at you* *as needing attention. These are the places that you need to look with conscious intention.*

> *"We have nothing to fear but fear itself."*
> Franklin Delano Roosevelt

FDR, 32nd president of the United States and the only president to be elected to four terms, noticed that during the Great Depression people were going into panic and it was impeding progress to get out of the current conditions.

First, we fear, then we want proof before we will let go of fear. One of the problems with this approach is that if we are in fear and creating from fear we are preventing the proof from being created. We are also preventing ourselves from noticing the proof when it is right in front of us. So many of us have beliefs that "We don't deserve," "We have to give before we can receive," "We deserve to be punished or to not get what we want," that we don't see how we are creating based on these unconscious beliefs and we continue to create more of what we don't want because it's what we think is true. Over time, your beliefs come true over and over for a few reasons:

1. *You unconsciously create from false beliefs that you believe are true.*
2. *The people around you are projecting onto you what they believe to be true and, on some level you go into agreement with them, therefore you are co-creating*

with them. *They may be family members, such as parents and siblings, who spoke these false beliefs over you from a young age.*

3. *Your beliefs are strengthened over time by the continuous recurrence of circumstances you have created that you develop more beliefs around your original false beliefs. You may have started by believing that you didn't deserve and now you believe that you are never going to get what you want and/or that God is a punitive God. Now what started out as "I don't deserve" has added that "I deserve to be punished" and by God. Since you are creating with the energy of the Divine you are able to bring to yourself what it is you believe. You show yourself what you believe by what you are creating.*

If we don't ask what something is all about we may make a story about it that is not accurate. Everywhere people are talking about finding out how to follow our inner guidance. If you google "inner guidance" 13,000,000 hits come up.

We misinterpret the meaning of things that are happening in our lives all the time. When we learn to use our intuition or inner guidance, we can ask questions to help ourselves make conscious choice.

Ready to evolve?

Exercise:

Ask yourself if how you are feeling is mental, emotional, spiritual or physical. Then ask if it is yours or someone else's.

If it is someone else's, you can ask to send that person love and support and make the statement "I consciously release the emotional energy of others" or "I consciously release collective stress."

If it is yours you can ask yourself what the deeper belief is that is creating what you are experiencing. If you are experiencing a seemingly negative feeling it is usually tied to a false belief that you can let go of after you discover what it is. To find this deeper belief, ask yourself what the feeling is? Identify the feeling. If you are having difficulty identifying the feeling, identify where in the body you are feeling this. This will usually help you to get in touch with what the feeling is. Contemplate this feeling. Have you felt this way before? How far back do you remember feeling this type of feeling? How do you think this started in your upbringing? What were the circumstances that you were living in that caused you to create a particular belief? What other beliefs do you feel you created as a result of the one you identified?

Example: If you have a belief that people will reject or abandon you then you may also have a belief that you don't get what you want. You may also have a belief in lack consciousness. You may also have a belief that you have to work hard. You may also have a belief that no matter how hard you work, you don't get what you want or that you can't have it all. These beliefs cause you to look around in your experience to prove them right or to prove yourself right. Then you are caught in a negative feedback loop creating the very thing you don't want to create but are creating because you have a belief or beliefs in what you are creating. You believe these things because you feel you have proof. You continue to create more proof. When we change our belief, we change our focus. We look for the proof in what we want rather than to prove ourselves right about what we don't want. The past does not dictate the future unless we believe that it does.

There are more complicated experiences that folks may need assistance to understand. Fortunately, there are many talented helpers out there who can help with uncovering the deeper issue and clearing, if necessary. I am grateful for the assistance I have received in helping me to uncover things I didn't know were possible and for looking in places I wouldn't have known to look. We are all meant to have H.O.P.E. – Heaven On Planet Earth and there is help for when we are struggling with that. I am grateful for the help I have received and for the H.O.P.E I have created from my work with Ashley Lee RN BSN Pediatric critical care nurse (Quantum Energy Healer and co-founder of Brain Integration Institute and Center for Conscious Kids), Donna Eden (Founder of Eden Energy Medicine), Bob Lee, PhD (Person-Centered Approach, studied directly under Carl Rogers) and many others who have helped me on my journey which had at times left me feeling that I didn't have HOPE. As we awaken, we help others to do the same. We show them that it is possible to come out of difficult circumstances, we show them how to find joy and we show them it is not only possible, but likely to realize our dreams.

We all need to help each other on this journey of being human. There are many moving targets and just when we think we have it all figured out something new comes into play. Things can happen that we didn't expect that change the course of our lives as we knew it. Some have a child that is born one gender but feels the other gender inside and wants to dress how they feel inside. Some people realize they want to be religious for the first time or they want to leave the church after a lifetime of dedication and explore other forms of spirituality, while others may decide that after all the years in law school and studying for the bar exam what they really want to do is something completely different. All are expressions of love incarnate. It doesn't matter WHAT we do, all that matters is that we stand in Love. When we allow love to guide the way all are included. Those that need love the most will receive the ripple effects of the love that is permeating the atmosphere around them. The folks with the most difficult behaviors are the ones that need the most help in the form of love. It may be that they need to be called out by witnesses who let them know that the world is changing and that kind of behavior is no longer acceptable. It is no longer acceptable to abuse children. A feeling of outrage may arise in many who read that statement insisting that abuse of children was never acceptable but the truth is that it was considered acceptable to "discipline" your own children however you saw fit as long as you were keeping them "under control." We are now recognizing that our beliefs that we project on others are highly impactful, especially on children. Children only want to help their parents. Children are often wiser about certain things than their parents. Parents who continue to carry the old model of parenting may feel threatened by a young one offering such wisdom in an effort to heal the relationship between parent and child. Conscious parents do not feel threatened by the wisdom of their little ones.

What we project on our children they will become. If we believe they are incapable of thinking for themselves, they will likely be incapable of thinking for themselves. If we believe that they have to be controlled they may rebel or not learn to think for themselves. If we believe they have to obey and not talk back they may learn to be covert and will have trouble in relationships throughout their lives as people pleasers or abusers because they weren't given choice. That is not a world created in Love. This is our history, but it is in the past. There are new patterns coming in to assist us in creating a world created in Love. People have the ability to grow, change and shift no matter their age. The old adage that "You can't teach an old dog new tricks" is no longer relevant. The "Helpers" in the field of science have proven that regardless of age well-worn neural pathways can change. Scientists have discovered ways to assist patterns in the brain change to create new pathways which can help prevent disease and cure addictions at the level of the brain. The term neuroplasticity describes the brain's ability to produce new neurons all the way until we die. The production of new neurons assists people in creating new habits.

> *"Neuroplasticity: The brain's ability to reorganize itself by forming new neural connections throughout life. Neuroplasticity allows the neurons (nerve cells) in the brain to compensate for injury and disease and to adjust their activities in response to new situations or to changes in their environment."*

> *Medical Author, William C. Shiel Jr. MD FACP FACR (Medicinenet.com)*

Many of us feel that our education system is antiquated and does not foster the innate gifts of the individual child. Prince Ea, a poet, eloquently elucidates through poetry on

YouTube the fact that our education system does not support bringing out the gifts and talents of each individual student. In one of his videos, he gave the example of how things have changed in the last 150 years. He shows pictures of how cars have changed, the telephone design has changed and how classrooms have not changed. In pictures he showed a classroom from 150 years ago and it looks exactly the same as classrooms today. Teachers are held to such strict standards within which they have to teach and it doesn't give them the freedom to use their own gifts and talents to teach students which could lift up individual students to find and foster their own unique talents.

CHAPTER 13

FAITH

Belief that is not based on proof.

*C*hange is a gift rather than something to fear. Having faith helps us continue on our path when we cannot see the road ahead. We weren't born into a perfect world, but a world that we are here to help. We are not separate from the spiritual world that is and always has been assisting us. We fear letting go of the past especially if we have created some measure of security for ourselves. Eckhart Tolle writes in his book "A New Earth":

> "There may be a period of insecurity and uncertainty. What should I do? As the ego is no longer running your life, the psychological need for external security, which is illusory

anyways, lessens. You are able to live with uncertainty, even enjoy it. When you become comfortable with uncertainty, infinite possibilities open up in your life. It means fear is no longer a dominant factor in what you do and no longer prevents you from taking action to initiate change. The Roman philosopher Tacitus rightly observed that "The desire for safety stands against every great and noble enterprise". If uncertainty is unacceptable to you it turns into fear. If it is perfectly acceptable it turns into increased aliveness, alertness and creativity.

Many years ago, as a result of a strong inner impulse, I walked out of an academic career that the world would have called "promising," stepping into complete uncertainty; and, out of that, after several years, emerged my new incarnation as a spiritual teacher. Much later, something similar happened again. The impulse came to give up my home in England and move to the West Coast of North America. I obeyed that impulse, although I didn't know the reason for it. Out of that move into uncertainty came The Power of Now, most of which was written in California and British Columbia while I didn't have a home of my own. I had virtually no income and lived on my savings, which were quickly running out. In fact, everything fell into place beautifully. I ran out of money just when I was getting close to finish writing. I bought a lottery ticket and won 1,000 dollars which kept me going for another month."

(A New Earth, 274 – 275).

This kind of action takes trust, faith and a strong sense of following your instincts. It isn't popular to take these sorts of risks. This experience can serve to make the insecurity stronger when those around us speak to the doubts you are already feeling about the uncertainty of the future. Most of us are well versed in "making sure" to choose the safest route and we are applauded when we do so. People see what they want to see. People don't ask, what risks did you take this year? How far will you go to follow your dreams? When you are fully ensconced in your purpose it is a fulfillment that cannot be compared to what we create out of duty or obligation or training. We hide behind the mask of success as defined by the world. As long as we make it look like what everyone thinks is successful and keep what isn't pretty "behind closed doors" we keep this thing going that is not fulfilling in the deepest sense. We push aside anything that doesn't fit into whatever it is we are "trying" to create. There is nothing wrong with wanting a good life *for ourselves but sometimes the lines are blurred between what we think we want and what our heart wants.*

You may ignore the deeper longings in your heart because these longings don't appear to fit into the life you are creating based on what you think you want. Unless you are listening with a deeper awareness the deeper longing of your heart may seem unrealistic. Part of what may cause unease is the unknown aspect of the calling. Unless you are being called to do something specific like go to medical school, your calling may feel like a less than secure path with many unknowns along the way. We come from generations, in the recent past, who were dealing with a lot of fear about survival and security having lived through times of uncertainty in history. In addition, we continue to get better at grooming ourselves and our children for success in the world as defined by the world. We know how to go to school and take tests. We know how to do what is expected of us in an effort to be accepted to the best schools and offered the best jobs.

We have created a world that we know how to navigate. What we do not know how to navigate is the unknown. We don't know the rules or how to follow them. We don't know how to make decisions in the unknown. If you learn about the most successful billionaires on the planet you will find that they were decisive and took risks. They made decisions and stuck with them. They made decisions and did not change their minds. We do ourselves a disservice when we second guess our choices and when we doubt ourselves.

There is an old saying regarding test taking to trust your gut and go with the first answer that comes to your mind and not second guess or change your answer. Following your instincts requires commitment and follow through. No one else is being guided to do exactly what you are doing and in exactly the same way. Only you know what is the right path for yourself and even if you ask 10 of your friends and family if they feel you are doing the right thing it will not be possible for them to know your truth or the truth of your calling in the way that you do.

If you have one person in your life who is able to hold the space for you while you talk about what you are going through, this will be a valuable relationship for you as you are going through transitioning to greater awareness and a more enlightened way of being in the world. One person who does not feel threatened by your different way of thinking and the potential changes that you are making. One person who doesn't feel compelled to give you advice but who can listen deeply and ask questions. You become investigators into the process of transformation in which you are undergoing. It is nearly impossible for this other person to not experience their own transformation as well while holding the space for yours. You both will have many Aha! moments as you uncover the deeper truths during your moments of inquiry. Just when you think you "know," something new will be ushered in that requires further investigation. There will be moments where strong feelings are experienced as a result of the letting go that you are choosing after a new truth is uncovered. In the Marvel movie "Dr. Strange," Benedict Cumberbatch's character does an excellent job portraying the metamorphosis of a very successful surgeon into a being of deeper awareness and deeper understanding about life and the presence of the unseen world. Although it is science fiction there is truth in the experiences human beings have when they choose to raise their conscious awareness. Much like in the movie where he is asked to expand his mind to include what he had previously considered impossible, so are we asked to expand our minds to include as possibilities what we have previously considered impossibilities. Resistance may arise in us if we do not approach this with trust and faith.

CHAPTER 14

SERVICE

An act of helpful activity; help; aid.

"For where two or three of you gather together in My name, I am there among them."

Matthew 18:20

"Where two or more of you are gathered in his name, there is love there is love."
"The Wedding Song"
by Peter, Paul and Mary

O*n your path of deepening awareness, having someone of like mindedness with you helps open up a greater love through your discussions and sharing of* experiences when you both value the purpose of opening to Love. Although you may experience periods of doubt and moments of loss of faith, having a friend or family member with whom you can share what you are experiencing will help provide support and reassurance. When you can say things that you know would sound crazy to some, and be met with understanding, you experience support stepping into the new. If you only have one person with whom you can share this process, that is enough. As more and more people are awakening, there will be more opportunities to grow communities of like-minded individuals. There are more and more groups being formed providing support for one another on the journey of awakening. They come together for strength and to refuel so they can go back out in the world and continue growing and bringing their gifts. These groups have the specific purpose of supporting each individual who would like support shifting to the new consciousness. Folks are able to grapple together as they navigate new territory discovering the gifts of the unknown. Each success will be a celebration for the group as each discovery of how to navigate the path of raising conscious awareness is shared.

The message of Jesus is that Love is The Way. Forgiveness is The Way. When we forgive ourselves for not knowing, for not loving ourselves, we open the door to Love. When we stand as witnesses to the truth about each other in Love, we open the door to Love. When we gather together to support each other we hold the door open until each of *us is firmly rooted. When we are rooted in love we are in Service to Us.*

In Service to Us, we change the landscape of the planet. Everyone is included in the abundance of resources our planet offers us. Everyone is also involved in taking care of our planet so that it can continue to render abundant. Everyone having food and shelter and education doesn't take anything away from anyone. It makes our world a better place, a more loving place, a kinder place. Our purpose is two-fold. It is to heal ourselves and our own lives and in doing so to heal our families, communities and ultimately our world. We can let go of old programming that includes our beliefs that others and life circumstances are responsible for our feelings. When we remember who we really are the projections of others no longer have an effect on us because we no longer agree with these false beliefs. People can think what they want to think about us but it doesn't affect us as we are on our way in Love. Folk's projections affect individuals as well as groups, countries, societies and any "other" that we deem separate from us. If the people receiving the projections are not strongly rooted in Love and the truth of who they are, they are vulnerable. We are being guided to be witnesses for those who aren't yet able to witness for themselves. When we serve as a beacon of light, we connect with the light in others. You may be the first or only person to see this for another.

What would it take for all of us to know the truth about ourselves? What would it take to release past wounding and therefore all the false beliefs we have taught ourselves, so that we can accept the truth of who we are--made from Love at the deepest part of our being.

There are many on the planet right now who are holding the space for this to come into everyone's consciousness. When you see this for yourself, you join in this collective vision. You see that in this field of consciousness, all is possible.

In Matthew 18:20 before he speaks about two or more gathering, the verse states: "Again, I tell you truly that if two of you on the earth agree about anything you ask for, it will be done for you by My Father in heaven."

CHAPTER 15

STILLNESS

Silence, quiet; hush.

S *itting in stillness allows our feelings to come to the surface.*

It is important that we take some time to quiet our minds and allow ourselves to experience everything we are feeling. Take the time to discover if we feel anxious and ask what is the root cause, if we feel depressed and ask what is the root cause, if we feel angry or agitated and ask what is the root cause. It is important to know if what you are feeling is yours or if what you are feeling is someone else's. If it is someone else's feelings then why are you holding them? What is your relationship with this person and what would cause you to feel what they are feeling? Is there something you want from them, which could include something you want them to do or something you want that they do not do? Do you carry a belief about relationships that is causing you to feel responsible for what the other is experiencing? Do you focus on trying to control others behaviors as a means of managing your own anxiety? Do you avoid how you feel in relationship to others so you don't have to find out what you are feeling?

We develop ways of relating to others and the world when we are very young. Children are egocentric and experience the world as if they are the center of it. Therefore, they are likely to feel that they have something to do with their parent's behaviors. They are geared towards figuring out ways to get their needs met if they are not getting what they feel they need. Every child wants and needs Love. Being seen, heard and understood is a big part of a child getting their needs met. Children are very intelligent and study what works and what doesn't work in an effort to get what they need from their parents. When they find something that they feel is working they keep doing it and therefore develop a habit. When there is no love in the family, a child decides that what is there is love because for there to be no love is intolerable for a child. A child might explain to herself that if she had not done something she would have received love, therefore blaming herself for not receiving the love that she needs. A child may also tell herself that she needs to do this thing or that thing and then she will be loved, therefore explaining to herself that the love is coming in the future. She is teaching herself that she has to give before she can receive. She is also teaching herself that she is not good enough just as she is, that she has to do something to earn love. This child will develop beliefs that are stored in her unconscious that will continue to dictate her relationships for the rest of her life or until she uncovers and releases them. She has now stored in her unconscious the beliefs that she is not worthy of love just as she is and that love is earned. If love is earned it can also be taken away. Other beliefs are then created around the original beliefs because they are related to the issue. As the child continues to develop and have experiences, these beliefs inform her to explain people's behavior and also to explain circumstances in the child's life. Therefore, these false beliefs, that were created in an effort to get one's needs for Love met, continue to get reinforced. As the reinforcement continues throughout one's life there is much evidence to support the truth of the belief. This pattern of looking at the world and relationships continues to bury the truth of who she is and the fact that she was never separated from Love.

A child may decide that she feels loved in certain situations where she feels her parent's approval therefore she will do what she feels is required. Getting good grades may be impressed upon a child who then learns to be pleasing by getting good grades in order to get love. If there is chaos in a family, a child will learn to pay more attention to how others are feeling than to her own feelings so that she will be able to determine how she should behave in an effort to get her needs for safety (and therefore Love) met. This child learns to push aside how she is feeling at a young age. When you teach yourself certain habits or ways of coping at a young age you don't realize consciously what you are doing and therefore take these habits with you into adulthood and carry them long past the time you live with your parents. You may continue to do what your parents did to you until you recognize what you are doing and consciously change the habit. If your parents were critical of you, you may continue to be critical of yourself. If your parents withheld approval until you did what they wanted you may withhold love from yourself or others.

Know thyself is one of the most important things you can do. To understand who you are and what beliefs you have which cause you to do the things you do is the key to opening the prison door that isn't even locked. It is the key to finding out what it is you don't know about yourself. You don't know what you don't know but it is your responsibility to find out what that is. All of us have free will and will feel a certain level of discomfort if we choose not to look. When we are standing in the energy of Love and Peace we don't feel as attached to what we thought we were attached to. Before we begin to experience glimpses of this, we don't see that we will feel ok. The more deeply ingrained you are in our habits and thought patterns, the more difficult it is to open up to the possibilities. Many have done research that points to the explanation that your thoughts, your fears, your beliefs can create physical illness. Bruce Lipton has done much research on this subject and identified how our cells change themselves based on our thoughts and intentions. How you feel about your circumstances is also rooted in your thoughts and beliefs. There are examples in history of people who were in extreme circumstances who survived largely due to accessing the stillness inside of them. In the movie "Invictus" about the life of Nelson Mandela, Morgan Freeman who plays Nelson Mandela, reads a poem which resonated with Nelson Mandela during his nearly thirty years of imprisonment doing hard labor in South Africa.

"Invictus" by William Ernest Henley 1888

Out of the night that covers me,
Black as the Pit from pole to pole,
I thank whatever gods may be
For my unconquerable soul.

In the fell clutch of circumstance
I have not winced nor cried aloud.
Under the bludgeonings of chance
My head is bloody, but unbowed.

Beyond this place of wrath and tears
Looms but the Horror of the shade,
And the menace of the years
Finds, and shall find, me unafraid.

It matters not how straight the gate,
How charged with punishments the scroll.
I am the master of my fate:
I am the captain of my soul.

Many have made discoveries for us about the Truth of who we are. They have done research in laboratories and in their careers or made discoveries as a result of their own extreme life circumstances. We don't have to reinvent the wheel by living out all of these different ways of discovering. We can investigate for ourselves the learning that has already been done. We can access the highest forms of Forgiveness and Love from the field that was created by those who have served as Witnesses for Truth. There is much that is a part of the Great Mystery but there is also much that we know to be true at the deepest part of our being. When we have released our unconscious triggers created in fear when we believed there was a lack of love, certain things begin to resonate with us even if there isn't any physical proof. We begin to see the Truth of Love in another. Seeing this in another, releases them from their belief in fear and in so doing, releases you.

You don't have to know exactly how to do this for yourself. There are many teachers, many books, many workshops, classes and helpers. If you ask for help it is given.

"Until one is committed, there is hesitancy, the chance to draw back, always ineffectiveness.

Concerning all acts of initiative (and creation), there is one elementary truth that ignorance of which kills countless ideas and splendid plans: that the moment one definitely commits oneself, then Providence moves too. All sorts of things help one that would never otherwise have occurred. A whole stream of events issues from the decision, raising in one's favour all manner of unforeseen incidents and meetings and material assistance, which no man could have dreamed would have come his way. Whatever you can do, or dream you can do, begin it. Boldness has genius, power and magic in it. Begin it now."

William Hutchison Murray

It is a bold act to face yourself and your fears. We don't even realize that we are not facing these things most of the time. We think we are doing our best and we are doing our best.

Most of us don't realize that we haven't "decided" to learn about ourselves. We think we already know ourselves. We know what happened in our childhoods and in our families while we were growing up. We know how we felt and what we want to pass on to our children and what we want to do better or remember not to do. We know that certain things get us a little upset or a lot. We think we probably know why these things happen. We can usually manage or find a way to distract ourselves until the feeling goes away. Or perhaps there are things that we don't really understand and we wish that others would understand that we have good hearts and good intentions as we act out certain behaviors that really do not reflect how we see ourselves. We are resigned that things are the way they are. We are resigned that we are the way that we are. However, we continue to feel anxious or depressed, sometimes a little or sometimes a lot. Sometimes we have a lot to unravel buried deep in childhood wounds or programming. Others may have gotten comfortable in their lives or are complacent but are being called to embrace and expand their true gifts they are here to give to the world. However, it is that you are experiencing your life and the world, all are called to the expansiveness of life through Love.

Ready to evolve?

Exercise: Write down your self-judgments. What is a self-judgment? A self-judgment is a conclusion we make about ourselves. An example might be: "I have to work in this job because nobody else will hire me".

When we discover what our self-judgments are we can release them. Why release self-judgements? Our self-judgments cause us to block manifesting what we want. Self-judgments are the same as beliefs and it is important for us to know how we are being unkind to ourselves by standing in judgment. Examples of self-judgments are:

> *I make mistakes*
> *I am judged*
> *I am irresponsible*
> *I am not enough*
> *I am not included*
> *I don't belong*
> *I can't change*
> *I can't change jobs*
> *I am not good at anything else*
> *I can't have it all*
> *It's too late*
> *I am too old*
> *I am broken*
> *Something is wrong with me*
> *I am a victim*
> *People don't like me*
> *I am stuck*
> *Things don't work out for me*
> *No matter what I do, things don't work out*
> *People owe me*
> *I am responsible*

It is my fault

People don't really care about me even though they say they do

I am not smart

I am not attractive

I don't deserve success

I can't handle it

If I look honestly at my feelings I will discover that what they say about me is true

If I look honestly at my feelings I will find out that something is wrong with me

I can't have what I want

Good things happen for others but not for me

I am not lucky

I have to work hard

I don't have enough time

I don't have enough money

Ready to evolve?

Exercise:

Self-judgments are usually underneath another feeling or thought.

   1. Notice a difficult feeling you are experiencing, then ask yourself what it is.

2. *After you identify what the feeling is, ask yourself what the self-judgment is underneath the feeling, if you don't already know.*

3. *Ask yourself if you would like to release this self-judgment and answer yourself with a clear answer of yes or no.*

4. *If yes, while feeling the difficult feeling of the judgment make the statement:*

   I consciously release the self-judgment that.......

5. *Then state I am now sovereign from this belief/self-judgment. (Even if it is temporary, it is good to experience this new energy).*

6. *Then state to yourself I am open to new perspectives about this judgement/situation.*

   Spend some quiet time inviting into your awareness what other perspectives there might be including the perspectives of others that you may not have originally considered.
   (Exercise inspired by Ashley Lee)

It is helpful to write down the self-judgements that you identify so that you can refer back to them when the feelings arise again. As you are in different situations or circumstances they may arise and you will be able more *easily identify them and release them. Over time they will not come back as frequently or at all. When you can't remember having had a particular self-judgment then you know it is gone.*

Notice yourself feeling more loving and accepting of yourself and your circumstances after doing this exercise. As you continue to release self-judgments on a daily basis, notice yourself adding more healthy choices to your self-care routine. These healthy choices may come in the form of stopping negative thought patterns, choosing to relate in healthier or more loving ways with those close to you or eating healthier and more.

Note: You will get clearer answers when you ask your guidance for help, after you clear your self-judgments.

CHAPTER 16

BEING

*The fact of existing; existence
(as opposed to non-existence).*

Throughout history, people have acted and reacted based on misunderstanding. When you don't feel free to speak openly with one another this causes suppression. In relationships if we interpret things a certain way that is wrong, and then act upon this false knowledge, we often create situations that lead to other situations we do not want. The same was and is true for relationships between countries and folks of differing religions. With the advent of mass communication, we have been able to dispel many misunderstandings about others and learn about cultures, religions, food and different types of lifestyles.

It is important that we get in touch with and know who

we are at the deepest level of our being-ness. The deeper we communicate with ourselves, the more we understand about life. We understand our relationships better and we better understand our life purpose. When we have better understanding, we are clearer when we communicate to others and take the time to clarify what others are communicating to us. We are better at recognizing that although someone may speak words that are familiar to us there can be differing meanings based on a person's life experience, age, economic status, mental state at the time, and culture to name a few. In addition, if an individual carries a particular type of energy ie., victim energy or demanding energy whether they know about it or not, we may react to that energy even if they are not outwardly acting it out. At the very least, it can be frustrating when we feel we are trying to communicate with others and are not being heard or understood. When our vibration is higher we speak in a language that resonates with most and we are able to feel/know the truth about a person or situation. Navigating in the world becomes easier for us. Our old ideas about the magic of life are transmuted into new understanding about The Great Mystery and our place in it.

As we are speaking clearly, we choose our words wisely knowing that each word has a very specific definition and vibration.

Definition:

   a. *A statement of the meaning of a word or word group or a sign or symbol.*

   b. *A statement expressing the essential nature of something.*

Vibration:

4a. A characteristic emanation, aura, or spirit that infuses or vitalizes someone or something and that can be instinctively sensed or experienced – often used in plural.

Merriam Webster Dictionary

The lowest form of communication is mindlessly throwing out words without paying attention. Our ability to attend to the way we communicate increases with in-depth self-awareness.

Self-awareness: An awareness of one's own personality or individuality.

When you know yourself, you learn to notice what you are feeling and why. You may choose to do some investigating about the root causes of how you feel, of old habits, of old beliefs. In your investigation, you may discover a deeper level of knowing about why you do the things you do, think the things you think and feel the things you feel.

With in-depth clarity about your own inner workings you are better able to free yourself from the chains that have bound you. You can reintegrate the parts of yourself that were forgotten or have been ignored. You may learn that there are many factors that may be affecting you and how to discern what is what.

With each issue you can ask:

Is this issue spiritual, mental, emotional or physical? Once you know then you can address the issue where it lives. It is helpful to have a guide, teacher, mentor or therapist who already knows how to do this for themselves to help you get started. I wasn't aware of this process until I met my teacher/healer/mentor/friend Ashley Lee. It doesn't have to take long with commitment and diligent action. We have conditioned ourselves to believe that psychological/ spiritual healing is a lengthy process. It is lengthy when it is not working. When you make a commitment to yourself and the process in combination with asking for help, what you need in that moment arrives. Each moment is a new moment and in each new moment as you continue to ask the help continues to arrive. As you create each moment you do so in that moment not striving for a finish line as much as trusting in the process. You are fulfilling your purpose each step along the way and making a difference in the lives of those around us. You are not waiting for some magical day when you have arrived at your purpose and have finally earned your worth. You matter now. Wherever you are in your journey, you matter now. If you are not yet feeling fulfilled in every area of your life, you matter now. You have a higher purpose at each stage of your development.

Even though we can't see how everything is being woven together we all have purpose at each moment and are contributing in Service to Us.

There is scientific evidence to support the fact that if we do our part we are greeted with support. Old habits to include old ways of thinking or well-worn neural pathways can be changed to new ways of thinking. We do not have to stay stuck in old thinking.

Neuroplasticity: 4. The capacity for continuous alteration of the neural pathways and synapses of the living brain and nervous system in response to experience or injury.

Our genes can also change when we change our thoughts and also our lifestyle moving away from stress. You can read more about this research in Bruce Lipton's books. His research proved that we are not victims of our genes that were passed down from our ancestors but can change our genes by making thought and lifestyle changes. We can heal ourselves and are not destined to get a disease just because our parents got it.

When we allow ourselves to have new experiences our brain responds in kind. Our bodies begin to change physically in response to new ways of thinking and ushering out old beliefs. Donna Eden, a leader in the field of Energy Medicine, states that all physical illness starts in the energy field before it becomes physical. She also states that we can heal ourselves as she did. Donna healed herself of a life-threatening illness when the Physicians told her there was nothing more they could do. Donna's experience lights the way for others providing proof that it is possible to heal ourselves. Not everyone has the gift of seeing energy the way Donna does. It isn't necessary to "see" energy to heal ourselves. You can learn from the teacher's that are here to help us. This is why it is so important that each of us share our gifts with the world. What if Donna had decided not to talk about what she experienced and about what she sees about self-healing?

What is it that we know about ourselves? We know that we can heal our physical bodies through changing our thoughts, beliefs and lifestyle. We know that we can heal ourselves psychologically by uncovering and releasing triggers. We know that if we pay attention to our emotions we will learn about our own beliefs that we created in childhood when we were abused or were not getting our needs met. We know that we sometimes have feelings that are not ours and that we can investigate what to do about them, and in the meantime, we can help ourselves by not making a story about feelings that are not ours. We know that nobody can do it for us and that there is help in abundance. When we are in our true essence of being-ness we know that we can ask for spiritual help and receive it and that we can access our Divine Guidance and intuition at any time. We know that our life matters at every step along the journey and that our gifts help at each stage of their development.

CHAPTER 17

EMPOWERED

To promote self-actualization or influence of.

*H*ow do you know if you are empowered? How do
you know if you are not empowered? Can you be
empowered in one or more aspects of your life but not in
others? Is it possible to take inspired action when you are not
empowered? You may want to ask yourself these questions
if you struggle finding the first steps toward creating the
life that you want. People who are not empowered have
reasons as to why they cannot reach their goals: too busy,
too tired, too many commitments, too many people counting
on them, not smart enough, what would people say, it's not
meant for me, maybe later, to name a few. When you are
not empowered, you have many reasons why you can't take
action. The first step towards any goal is to take an action

step. The moment you do this the universe shows up to help. The action step can be small like clearing the clutter in your house or catching yourself every time you have a negative or self-deprecating thought. Writing down your goals in increments of time starting with one month, one year, five years, ten years and then seeing what you can do now to take action steps towards those goals. Christie Sheldon talks about this in her "Love or Above" course. She recommends creating statements for yourself and saying them several times each day. "What would it take for me to have (insert goal here), and anything in the way of it delete, un-create and transmute." These statements are empowering because you are stating to the universe what you want and asking for help to achieve it.

Ready to evolve?

Exercise:

Write down what you would like your life to look like in one month, five years, ten years.

Then write down 3 action steps you can take for each goal.

You can refer back to these anytime.

Then state, as Christie Sheldon teaches, "What would it take for me to have (insert goal here) and anything in the way of it, delete, un-create and transmute.

"Faith is taking the first step even though you don't see the whole staircase."
"Power is the ability to achieve purpose. Power is the ability to affect change."

Martin Luther King Jr.

When you start to do something new you may feel uncomfortable because you are doing something different. This is usually a result of your past beliefs and fears coming up to be addressed. This is the opportune moment to uncover hidden beliefs and fears. It is your next action step. Sometimes what your heart wants isn't the path of least resistance. Sometimes what your heart wants requires you to grow and stretch in order to step into it. When you have asked and the universe answers, it begins with what needs to be cleared out of the way so that you can have, do, be what your heart wants. What your heart wants is guiding you to your purpose.

"Anyway" by Mother Teresa (original version by Kent M. Keith)

People are often unreasonable, illogical and self-centered; Forgive them anyway.
If you are successful, you will win some false friends and some true enemies; succeed anyway.

*If you are honest and frank, people may
    cheat you;*
Be honest and frank anyway.
*What you spend years building, someone
    could destroy overnight;*
Build anyway.
*If you find serenity and happiness, they may
    be jealous;*
Be happy anyway.
*The good you do today, people will often be
    forgotten tomorrow;*
Do good anyway.
*Give the world the best you have, it may
    never be enough;*
Give the world the best you've got anyway.
*You see, in the final analysis, it is between
    you and your God;*
It was never between you and them anyway.

*In the words of Mother Teresa, follow your
heart anyway.*

*"Would you like me to give you a formula for success?
It's quite simple, really: double your rate of failure. You
are thinking of failure as the enemy of success. But it isn't
at all. You can be discouraged by failure or you can learn
from it, so go ahead and make mistakes. Make all you*

can. Because remember that's where you will find success."
Thomas Watson, Sr. Chairman and CEO of IBM who
was largely responsible for the company's success and was
called the world's greatest salesman when he died in 1956.

"Intuition is loving guidance."
Louise Hay

How do we become unempowered?

This is a question that has been raised about entire
populations of people. When you are unable to be in your
own agency we are unempowered.

Agency: 2. :"the capacity, condition or state of acting or
of exerting power. Merriam-Webster dictionary."

When you are oppressed by conditions you experience an
inability to be in your own agency and thus in your own
power. If you are raised by parents who are not in their
own power you will learn that you do not have your own
power in the world. When you are raised in an abusive
environment you may learn that you do not have your own
power. When you are grown you have the ability to rise
above conditions. You have the ability to rise out of your
circumstances and stand in your own power. You may have
inherited beliefs in powerlessness from your ancestors that
were passed down to you through your parent's attitudes
and beliefs.

Your unconscious beliefs could be a result of your lack of agency. It is possible that underneath the false beliefs you created about your self-worth, about whether or not things work out for you or you get what you want could be rooted in an underlying belief that you do not have the power to create what you want or to create change.

When you realize and begin to utilize your connection to your higher self, you begin to empower yourself. You have a connection to Divine Guidance that can see what you cannot see, and that can help you to go in the direction of what it is that you want in Service to US. It is very empowering to know that you have inside you, a resource that will not let you down. You are born with this resource to guide you throughout your life so that you can express the highest form of your existence. You are already equipped with the resources you need to empower yourself. There are those who can help us to learn about this. There are those who can help us to learn about ourselves but ultimately, we are our own Guru. There isn't anyone who knows what is better for us than we know for ourselves. We are being guided to access the love that lives inside us, all around us and empower ourselves through our connection to our Divine resources to live the life that we were meant to live. We were meant to love and to be supported and to lift each other up. When you are consciously creating, what you want for yourself also serves the greater good. You are supported and guided to create what you want as it serves the greater good.

It is not selfish to want what you are wanting because if you obtain what you want and you do so consciously, you do so in Service to Us. When you want to build a successful company and you are doing so consciously, you create wealth which you then use to help lift others. You may be guided to employ your wealth by helping to educate people so that they can do the same. You may provide jobs that enable people to have freedom within their workspace to come in at flexible hours and to get ahead through profit sharing or other avenues. There are infinite ways that Divine Consciousness will guide each of us in the great unfolding of love on the planet.

Scientists are coming in to provide us with the proof that so many of us want. We want proof that "God" exists and that Love exists. Most of us and even those who consider themselves spiritual, have difficulty having Trust and Faith in the absence of proof. Most would like something to show them the proof of what they believe or feel is True. Some are better than others at reminding themselves daily that what they are experiencing as Love and Miracles is true. Others who may be running certain programs about victimization or suppression may experience more doubt and can use all the help they can get.

"Power is the ability to achieve purpose. Power is the ability to affect change."

MLK

There are psychological reasons as to why we do not empower ourselves. We may have beliefs that we are not good enough or that life is hard and we have to work hard before we can receive. We have beliefs that we don't deserve or that we can never get what we want. We have beliefs that we deserve to be punished and that it is selfish or not spiritual to have abundance. Some have beliefs that God is a punitive God or that we have to sacrifice ourselves for others. We believe in obligation and choosing duty to others or duty to country even if it doesn't feel like the right choice for our lives or what our heart wants. We believe in the patriarchy and matriarchy casting levels into our society which are assigned to each of us based on financial status, skin color, education level or level of success in our careers. When we believe in status we give others power over our lives. We ascribe doctors, clergy, the court system, the school system, and the monetary system/corporations a false power. We give ourselves over to these "experts" and those in a position of false power which further serves to disempower us. When we learn to listen to our intuition, or inner guidance we can empower ourselves to know if something is right for us rather than take the word of the "experts." If a physician is making a recommendation we can go inside and check with our inner guidance about whether or not it is the right choice for us. When making decisions for our children, regardless of the popular opinion, we can check with our "inner parenting knowledge" to assist us in making our choices. We are not in this alone and have, at our fingertips, assistance from a higher consciousness that has the ability to see the bigger picture and is not governed by fear. Why would you not choose to seek guidance from this vantage point?

You have free will and can choose what you want to choose. You need not go outside of yourself to ask what is right for you. Only you know what your soul needs. You empower yourself when you recognize that you are your own ultimate authority. You have resources to assist you in making choices that are for the true and highest good. You empower yourself when you release your conflicts as a result of the false beliefs you have created. We create beliefs that are not true about ourselves and life and then we judge people, places, circumstances and things based on these beliefs, which creates conflict. When we do conflict resolution within ourselves, we free ourselves from giving our power to people, places, circumstances and things that we fear have power over us which is why we judge and create the conflict.

We are making, what may seem to many as radical, shifts in our consciousness. There is evidence of these shifts in the open conversations we are having about subjects that were previously considered taboo such as transgender issues and homosexuality, sexual abuse and misconduct, the fact that there were several women running for president, that we are questioning our government and the way it is run, that we are allowing ourselves to see the systemic sickness that plagues our society, and that we are recognizing that *if we don't make some radical shifts there will be a rise in events such as terrorism and school shootings. Even though "freedom of speech" is in our Declaration of Independence, we haven't truly been free to speak about many things and as a result we have passively allowed the creation of a society where we still experience poverty, inequality, abuse, injustice, and disempowerment.*

It may be easy to not notice what is going on. If you are in the habit of focusing on the negative then that is what you will see; if you are in the habit of noticing the good that is going on around you, then that is what you will see. There is much chaos in the news and it could seem that we are not getting better, but getting worse. We need for all of us to witness not only the chaos but the truth of who we are and where we are going for things to change. We need to stand as witnesses for the love that is in all of us and therefore the ability to create change and lift up our world and our country through conscious choice no longer taking for granted that the truth lies in collective consciousness passed down by false beliefs. We are not only uncovering individual false beliefs in our unconscious but collective false beliefs in our collective unconscious. The individual is a microcosm of the macrocosm. I am witnessing in my practice, individuals who are uncovering false beliefs in their unconscious which is an indication there are others who are doing this. We are gaining momentum in our uncovering as more and more take responsibility for their experiences in their lives.

> *"Your inner purpose is to awaken. It is as simple as that. You share that purpose with every other person on the planet — because it is the purpose of humanity."*
>
> *Eckhart Tolle*

You are so much more "Ok" than you think. We are so hard on ourselves that we forget that we are OK. That way of thinking is also what keeps us disempowered. We continue to feed the belief that we have to fix something about ourselves or many things about ourselves before we can start to think of ourselves as ok. You are OK now. There was a book written in the 1960's entitled "I'm ok, You're ok." You are ok now even if you haven't arrived at the exact place you want to be in every area of your life. You can connect to your higher consciousness at any moment. You can receive guidance at any moment. You can let the lower parts of yourself know that you are grateful for all the ways in which they have tried to care for you but that you've got this. You can take the wheel from here. You are in charge, not your ego. Your ego can come along and can stay with you but you don't need it to take the reins anymore. Give it unconditional love and ask it to sit on the sidelines and watch as your life unfolds through your own choices guided by your Higher Consciousness and see what happens. Ask Higher Consciousness to guide you noting that it is You who are choosing to create your life now without interference by your ego. The ego cannot help but to create from a place of fear, lack, and insecurity. This is why you thank your ego and lovingly relieve it from its duties that it has done so well to the best of its abilities and let it know that you are now in charge. You want your ego to gracefully secede.

Your ego is rooted in fear. It can have good intentions. It can care about what is right and what is wrong. It can work hard and take care of its responsibilities. It can think that it is doing all the "right" things and deserves to be rewarded for its focus on duty and obligation but it is mistaken. The ego causes confusion and grief to its host who believes they are doing what they are supposed to do and believing what they are supposed to believe. Eventually, we find out that some things we believed were not true or were simply not right for us. The ego may have been invested in the outcome it expected for all it's hard work and may feel let down after having invested in certain beliefs. When you recognize that is what is happening you can let go of the old attachments. You free yourself by opening to new perspectives of how the old beliefs served you in the past but no longer serve you in the now.

CHAPTER 18

FORGIVENESS

Act of forgiving; state of being forgiven.

*W*hen we forgive we change the past.
    We have spent too much time and effort on "healing" ourselves when, in reality, what we need to do is to release anything that stands in the way of us allowing us to be ourselves. There is a line from a Leonard Cohen song that says, "ring the bells that still can ring, there is a crack in everything, that's how the light gets in." We have built barriers that block us from the truth of who we really are. When you practice forgiveness, you allow those barriers to crack. You will still remember what happened, but you can change how you view what happened. You can change how you view yourself in light of what happened. You can forgive the people or the situations and you can forgive

yourself for being a part of whatever it was that happened. I invite you to forgive yourself and to forgive others.

Ready to evolve? Write down specific situations that you still need to forgive.

Exercise:

I invite you to forgive the situations that happened that you feel grief about. If you say "yes I want to forgive," while holding in your mind the person and/or the situation or yourself, then you have forgiven and can now be free of what you were holding on to. You can release the other person or the situation from "owing" you anything. People often feel that others owe them something after they feel they have been "wronged." Sometimes the feeling of owing is unconscious. People may say that they have moved on from something but still hold in the unconscious that they are owed. Forgiving a person or a situation releases you from any feeling that someone or something "owes" you. This is empowering for you. It is empowering to know that no-one owes you anything and you have the power to create the life of which you dream. When you believe that someone owes you something you are more susceptible to the belief that you do not get what you want.

In order to create the life you want, you must first clear counter beliefs in your unconscious. You will then be able to create without an opposing force drawing in experiences that are contrary to what you want. When you do this, your life purpose and what you truly want to create for yourself andy our community becomes clear. You will no longer be bogged down by the projections of others or by unconscious beliefs. You take responsibility for what is yours and forgive what is not. You are no longer triggered in all the ways you used to get triggered by perceived wrongdoings of others. you no longer take personally the actions of others. You forgive your judgments of others and by uncovering the beliefs that precipitated your judgments, you release your propensity to judge.

"What is HO'OPONOPONO? And how does it help?

Ho'oponopono is an ancient Hawaiian practice still in use today and is well-known for the miracle it does in clearing negativity from one's mind and thought. It is believed to be designed to wipe out all the negativity in our thoughts and those blocks that are keeping us miserable. Dr. Joe Vitale is a renowned Ho'oponopono creator and practitioner; the author says that there are a large number of us who don't have the luxury of enjoying peace, harmony or joy forever in our lives. It is believed that external negativity plays a role and we are saddled right from birth. And this Hawaiian technique Ho'oponopono has been specifically designed to remove all the stress and negativity from our minds and let us enjoy eternal happiness forever. It is a simple technique where one asks for forgiveness and purifies oneself.

What is Ho'oponopono remedy that works so well and takes away all your guilt? The answer to this question can be discussed through the four steps of performing Ho'oponopono.

There are four phases or steps that the practitioner can follow and the magical healing starts from within. The four steps involved in this practice make you realize the fact that you are responsible for everything that happens to you and that is in your mind. Once you realize this fact it becomes easy for you to start practicing the steps.

1. *The first step asks you to say sorry for everything that has happened or any wrong thing that you have witnessed. It makes it easy for you to move ahead in your life once you know the fact and have the courage to say sorry for anything that was wrong, you will feel better.*

2. *Once you are able to say sorry the second step requires you to ask for forgiveness. You will be seeking forgiveness for everything you felt sorry for in the first step. While doing so, you are asking to forgive everything from you and your past memories that may have been involved in the wrong doing. These*

may sound weird for many of us but once you mean what you say the process is magical.

3. *The third step that you must go through is showing your gratitude for everything that has happened to your life. This way you will learn to appreciate everything that is big or small in your life. You might get an unexpected response for this thank you but you need not worry about the result or response. In the right time the correct result will appear in front of you. This step will help you to have patience as well.*

4. *The last step you need to follow is to show your love and say I love you to everything that is yours. That way you will learn to love everything related to you". – Joe Vitale*

(From joevitalehooponopono.com)

It may not always be possible or necessary for you to speak words of forgiveness in person. It is still a valuable process to do on your own as you practice recognizing your judgements and releasing them. When we judge, we are doing so based on a belief that we carry either in the conscious or in our unconscious mind. To truly shift into a higher level of consciousness we illuminate our beliefs that cause us to create judgments, thus ushering in conscious choice. We are always in choice. We can either choose from unconscious motives or from conscious. The more we know about ourselves and the more we take responsibility we are then able to usher in conscious choice.

"Mitakuye Oyasin" is a prayer from the Lakota Sioux which means to honor the union with the Spirit, with oneself, with other people, with nature and with the Creator as we are all Related. And so it is. (This passage is from a meme on Facebook.)

My hope in writing this book is to provide people with enough evidence about what is being offered to us in as many ways possible, to help us raise our consciousness and stand in conscious choice. My goal is to expose readers to an array of what is out there. I have spent many years researching, at first because I was interested then I became fascinated then it was out of necessity through the pain of my own transformation. It is only a belief that letting go has to be painful or that changing or shifting has to be hard work. It is a belief that is very common and so it is that we go about transforming through pain. This is changing now as we begin to recognize the truth of who we are and that we create how we want to experience ourselves in this human existence. As we practice uncovering our beliefs, we are able to recognize the beliefs that are buried and oftentimes, subtle.

When presented with simple practices for profound change we doubt that it can be that easy. We think with our linear minds, we judge without first checking to see what it is all about. We may notice resistance to opening *our minds to new ways of looking at ourselves. It is a challenge for people who have mental rigidity or who have felt that they are a victim and wonder how they could possibly be responsible for anything that has happened in their lives, to shift to open mindedness. These folks may find it challenging to do simple exercises to release regret, judgements and old beliefs. It is a challenge to do a simple exercise in conflict resolution when one is accustomed to it either being everyone else's fault or always their fault. If those are the only two choices then it will be a challenge to do a simple exercise in releasing conflict. The challenge doesn't come from participating in hard tasks in the outside world. The challenge comes from going within. It isn't easy to shift from seeing the world in linear terms to seeing that we are not linear beings and that the world is not linear, even if it looks that way.*

Ready to evolve?
Exercise:

Identify and then write down regrets that come to mind.

Write down the reasons that you feel you made the decisions you made at that time.

Many people feel regret when they begin to awaken. They feel regret for what could have been and for choices they made in the past. One way to heal through the regret is to extend empathy for our past self that made the choices that were made.

Think of the situation for which you are feeling regret. Then think of what you got from that situation. Notice where you come from and why someone who comes from where you come from would have made the choices you made.

Ask yourself if you can understand why someone who comes from this place would have made the choices you made?

Give yourself love.

It can be helpful to talk about it with a trusted individual who knows your history. You will know if you have addressed this past regret if you find that you can't recall the same feeling of regret that you felt. Notice if you feel differently as you try to remember what you felt regret about and what you felt you had gotten from the situation. The past changes as you grow and change. The facts might stay the same but the feeling and the story around what happened changes.

CHAPTER 19

PSYCHOLOGY

The science of the mind or of mental states and processes.

*O*ur psychology is an important aspect of ourselves. When we work with ourselves inside of a psychological framework, we have available to us methods that have been researched and proven effective.

While I was in graduate school, I was fortunate to meet a Psychologist whom I chose to be my mentor through my graduate program in psychology. Dr. Robert Lee learned the person-centered approach directly from Carl Rogers and I learned it from him. This style spoke to me even before I knew anything about what was healing and I was fortunate enough to be referred to him by one of my graduate professors. At the time, I am not sure I understood *what that meant. I had some idea that it was about taking responsibility for ourselves after being held in a safe and loving container by the therapist, but now I have a much clearer picture about what this practice entails. It is no longer just a concept to me. With the person-centered approach, it is a collaborative effort on the part of client and therapist to help expand the views of the past by loosening up the client's stories. Instead of continuing throughout people's lives to tell their stories as if they happened yesterday, we work together to understand their stories at deeper and deeper levels. Clients then shift in their awareness of their experience and their past no longer holds the charge it once did. One way that I have found to do this is, to uncover judgements and beliefs. When they find their judgements and release their core beliefs underneath them, that are not true, clients experience profound shifts.*

There are many experts in the field on conflict resolution and I do not claim to be one of them. However, from the perspective of a counselor in psychology I have experienced first-hand and witnessed in others that much of the conflict starts at the level of the individual. If we can address the conflicts within ourselves we can heal the world.

When you address the conflicts you have in relationships, or with places or circumstances, you are uncovering the conflicts you have within yourself. The conflicts originate within yourself even though you may feel that is not the case.

We are neither completely at fault, nor are we completely without a part in the conflict. For example,

> *You have a belief that you do not deserve to be forgiven.*
>
> *You have another belief that you deserve to be punished.*
>
> *You are having a conflict with your significant other who feels you are doing something that you are not doing or have not done.*
>
> *You have a discussion with your partner who feels they cannot let it go and it feels confusing to you that they won't let it go. You have given all the evidence and explained this is not what you are doing.*
>
> *Your partner doesn't feel they can forgive you whether you have done it or not and may not understand why they feel this way.*
>
> *The reason they can't forgive you for what they judged you for is because you have already stated to the universe that you are not to be forgiven.*
>
> *The partner is also reacting because they have their own beliefs about forgiveness or about punishment. They are going into agreement with you that you are not to be forgiven.*

Do you see how you have essentially done nothing in this scenario but are contributing to the conflict by having an untrue belief about yourself that doesn't allow another to resolve the conflict by forgiving you? We paint ourselves into a box with our beliefs that do not let us out. We have beliefs about God that keep us suppressed because if we believe that God does not forgive us for certain things and we have done that certain thing then there is no hope. We may not even realize what our beliefs are about God because we have hidden them from ourselves so we cannot even locate what it is that is preventing us from resolving the conflict. If we cannot resolve the conflicts within ourselves, we cannot realize our full potential which is the same as realizing our dreams. If we continue to suppress ourselves with untrue beliefs that keep us creating conflicts because we are judging people, places, circumstances and things, we will not be able to reach our full potential. When you take responsibility for your part in every area of your life, you become free. Things that used to have a charge when you thought about them, no longer have a charge. You will have the ability to feel all of your feelings and move through them with Grace. You don't hold on to stories that no longer hold weight. You see that they were here to teach you something about yourself. Yes, we were innocent children when we first started creating our beliefs about life. For many who were a mistreated innocent child, it wasn't right what was done to you. Yet, it is only you who can uncover what you have conflicts with and find the beliefs underneath the conflicts and release them. You may never get an apology for the abuse, or for never having gotten your needs met, AND you can free yourself. You can free yourself from the state of victimhood. You can free yourself from limiting beliefs about life. You can free yourself from limiting beliefs about yourself, about relationships and about your value in the world. You may have to first free yourself from your resistance to believing that this is possible. We are guided to forgive the judgments of the person who did the wrongdoing, not the hurtful behavior, to forgive the wrong thinking. This is to free YOU! The truth is that there is a part of you that was never touched, that remains intact, that has witnessed everything you have gone through. You can access that part now.

Conversely, you may feel that you don't have many issues and that it is more everyone else that is creating or participating in conflict. In the past, I thought that the best way to resolve conflict was not to participate in it. I didn't have good role models for conflict resolution when I was growing up. Later, I realized that avoiding conflict actually creates it. People avoid difficult feelings who are avoiding conflict. Many are also avoiding their own difficult feelings who are creating conflict by blaming others for the way they feel. Usually, those difficult feelings are about yourself and your own life. We are then not able to have deeper feelings and therefore deeper connections with the people in our lives. We are not being true to ourselves by avoiding conflict because we are doing what we think is the "right thing" to avoid conflict. As I described in the example above, there is usually some way that we are "participating" without realizing it. At the very least, we may be needed to state to the other that how they are behaving towards us or what they are asking of us is not ok. An example might be a person who goes to law school because his parents decided that that is what they want for their son even if he knows that is not what he wants to do. Eventually, he will realize that he chose law school to avoid conflict and will get to a point when he can no longer avoid the conflict within himself regarding the choice he made. Another example could be a couple who doesn't tell each other how they really feel and it goes on for years and suddenly one of them walks away from the marriage with no warning, leaving the other feeling blindsided. The person who avoids conflict doesn't want to hurt the others feelings therefore having to face one's own discomfort, while growing increasingly distant until one day they could not keep up the façade any longer and walked away. I have worked with couples who feel that they cannot trust their "conflict avoiding" partner. Instead of saying how they really feel, they looked outside the marriage to friends or other members of the family to get their needs met. People avoid conflict because they have fears based on beliefs they have about themselves and about life. Whether you are the one outwardly creating the conflict or you are avoiding it, you have a conflict and a belief beneath it. Releasing the belief will free you even if the other person or people haven't released the conflict for themselves. It can be fascinating to watch the miracles that occur in others when you release the conflict inside yourself. I have had experiences releasing conflict in my own relationships that I, in the past, had little to no hope that anything would get better only to find that miracles happened and people didn't react to the situation based on past behaviors. Watch for the miracles when you do this!

Most of us do not realize how much conflict we are in and have been in for most of our lives. We have conflict with religion, politics, institutions, parenting, parents, concepts such as: entitlement, disappointment, arrogance, judgement (we have judgement about judgement); child abuse, sexual abuse, rape, slavery, health care, health, our bodies, marriage, being single, child rearing, life, education, government, the president, other countries, cultures, what is expected of us, money, food, exercise, cars, traffic, weather, nature, the earth, and we have conflict with people who uphold all these conflicts.

We have conflict with ourselves for who we think we are not, for choices we have made, for our beliefs that we are not worthy or deserving, or forgivable, or likeable, or loved. The hard part in releasing the blocks to success or to living a life of fulfillment is not releasing the blocks. In my experience, the hard part is in getting to know that we have these blocks and then getting to a place of willingness inside of ourselves to release these blocks. The actual releasing happens with ease.

Ready to evolve?

Exercise:

Identify a belief that you would like to change.

Write down at least 3 beliefs about yourself that you can identify.

Feel - the feeling of this belief.

Ask - Would I like to release this belief?

State - "I consciously release the belief that…..".

While doing this it is important to focus on the feeling of the issue that you are releasing. It is not enough to simply repeat words without the felt sense of what you are releasing.

> *State – I am sovereign from this belief.*
>
> *State – I open to new perspectives.*
>
> *Feel – Feel what it feels like to be sovereign from the belief and to be open to new perspectives. Imagine what these new perspectives might be.*
>
> *(Inspired by Ashley Lee)*

Another way to get clear about how you are feeling is by getting centered, grounded, and in a true place of willingness to see how you have created your life in part and as a result of judgments you had due to false beliefs. We hold the beliefs that it has to take time, be difficult or strenuous, and that we can't have it all which creates blocks. You can help yourself by replacing your old thoughts patterns with new thoughts such as, "All the world is conspiring in my favor in every area of my life." Focused attention on positive thoughts will help neuroplasticity replace the old brain patterns with new ones created in gratitude and hopefulness. When you don't have unconscious beliefs creating circumstances in your life, you have the freedom to consciously create.

First, you clear yourself, then you contribute to the betterment of humanity and the planet by standing in love and doing your purpose as you are guided to do by your higher self. Clearing yourself which requires focus and dedication takes time and may seem selfish to some who do not understand.

I read an article on Facebook by David Daniel Brown. This is what he wrote:

How to care for a shedding human.

Humans shed regularly throughout their life to enable growth. Shedding usually takes as long as it fucking takes. Although this is a completely natural process, there are certain steps you can take to care for a shedding human. Make sure you foster a hospitable environment for the human by adding extra love and compassion. Remind the human that any discomfort is normal and will lessen soon after change. If you notice any complications, such as fear and self-sabotage, stand up for the human. Do not ignore the human. Encourage and stand beside the human. Hold a sign. Light a candle. Cause a ruckus. Drag them into any sunlight available. Sing to them. Bring them unnecessary cookies. Hold their hand. Whisper good things in their ears. Kiss them a little. Tell them the story of your shedding. The beautiful and exquisitely painful ways you've changed too. Repeat forever. ATS

I often refer to this process as recalibrating or going through a transformation. It is nothing to be ashamed of as it's not always a guarantee that everyone will understand what you are going through. Do it anyway. Unfortunately, no-one can do it for you nor can you do it for anyone else. There may be people whom you feel judge you because they don't have all the information and do not understand your choices. Transform anyway. You don't owe anyone an explanation for your choices, you simply need to make choices that YOU are guided to make.

It is an easy formula for releasing triggers to notice when you have a conflict and acknowledge the conflict. Then find the belief underneath the conflict and release the belief. As you change in this way and are taking responsibility for most things in your life, the people who are no longer right for you may fall away from your life. You won't have to weed people out, they will just stop calling, coming by or inviting you. Do not be offended. They were important in your unfolding and you can honor that. You can honor them for they have their own journey that is just as important as yours. You can wish them well.

I saw a brief video of Marianne Williamson on Oprah's Super Soul Sunday. They were talking about forgiveness. Marianne said, and was referring to a Course in Miracles, that the blueprint of the best possible manifestation of your life is already in existence and all you/we need to do is download it. If you are in bitterness from not forgiving, you are downloading bitterness. If you pray for the person you have a conflict with for 30 days, you are using divine alchemy to transform the energy within yourself. The message I received from listening to Marianne is that when you clear away what you do not want to download then you can download the higher possibilities for your life that are already in existence. It is waiting for you to step into what is meant for you. All the world is conspiring in your favor in every area of your life.

Ready to evolve?

Exercise:

Identify if you have bitterness from not forgiving. Say a prayer for the person or the situation you felt you could not forgive. Repeat for 30 days. Notice how you feel throughout the process and after 30 days. Write it down so you can refer to it later.

There are infinite ways that our lives can unfold for the greater good. All of these ways lead us to living fulfilling lives in Service to Us. In the book Power vs. Force, Dr. Hawkins states that when we are vibrating above a certain level our vibration contributes to and makes up for a certain number of people who are vibrating at lower levels. You are helping by vibrating higher. When people vibrating at lower levels receive energetic support they are more likely to raise their own vibrations. Acknowledging conflict and releasing beliefs helps you to access the blueprint of your best life which helps make the world a better place. And you get to feel better! Imagine if everyone was doing this how quickly we would raise the consciousness of the planet? As we express the highest possible manifestation of our life in each moment the next possibility comes in for us to express. This must also be true for humanity. As humanity expresses the highest possible manifestation of itself then the next higher expression is then made available to us. We are able to bring into Being-ness higher levels of consciousness ultimately bringing more Peace to our world.

CHAPTER 20

UNCONSCIOUS

*Not perceived at the level of
awareness; occurring below the
level of conscious thought.*

*C*learing beliefs can be challenging if you don't know how
to access the ones that are in your unconscious. For those
who are not accustomed to self-testing, meditation can be a
good way to unlock the beliefs that are in the unconscious mind.

Ready to evolve?

Exercise:

Choose a time when you can relax and focus on sitting
in a quiet space. Find a comfortable position and take a
few deep breaths. Tap your cheek bones below your eyes.

Put your hand above your head first with palm side down then switch to palm side up. Switch back and forth several times.

(This is an energy medicine technique taught by Donna Eden. Both sides of our hands have polarities like a magnet. We are opening your channel that connects you to "above.") When we doubt or ask "why," we disconnect ourselves spiritually. This is an easy exercise to open up that flow.

Tapping your cheek bones, also taught by Donna, is a good way to get grounded by tapping these points on stomach meridian. Other ways Donna teaches for grounding include walking barefoot in the grass, rubbing the bottom of your feet with a stainless-steel spoon, leaning on a tree or walking in the ocean)

Now that you are grounded and connected from above, ask to be connected to higher consciousness.

Envision a white or golden light flowing down from above and entering at the top of your head and completely filling you up all the way down to your toes and rooting you into the ground. Continue taking a few more deep breaths while you envision being filled up with this light.

Next, create a place in your mind where you would like to receive guidance ie., a garden, a meadow, a beach, or whatever comes to your mind.

Then, ask your guidance to show you your unconscious beliefs. You can say: I am open to knowing my unconscious beliefs. If you are not accustomed to receiving information in this way, be patient, it will come. It may come in the form of a thought or feeling, or a picture, or an idea about something. Different people receive guidance differently, therefore you will also be learning how you receive guidance.

Another way that I use to get in touch with unconscious beliefs is by noticing. I notice when I am feeling something which feels incongruent. Incongruence can occur in the form of anxiety or an uncomfortable feeling. I used to feel insecure because I was feeling uncomfortable and my self-talk would take over telling myself that something was WRONG with me. Now I notice how I am feeling when I am uncomfortable and ask questions about it. My "self" at the age I am now has changed particular beliefs I had in the past. There are times that a part of me lets me know that there is something in my unconscious from the past, by sending me signals through feelings of discomfort. In that situation I know I have something to investigate. It is not the situation, it is not the people I am with, and it is not the fact that there is something wrong with me. It's a belief or self-judgment. When I learned to look at how I was feeling in this way, it felt freeing. I have the ability to identify what I am feeling and I have tools in my toolbox to address it if I need help.

When you listen to your self-talk you find unconscious beliefs through what you tell yourself. I had a client who experienced frequent migraines. One day she started listening to her self-talk in the midst of a migraine. She was telling herself that she didn't know what she needed and that there was no-one who could help her. She was getting in touch with past trauma and how she had felt each time this trauma had occurred. This self-talk was showing her wounds that were yet unhealed and ready to be addressed. I encouraged her to thank this part of herself for having the courage to bring this to her attention so that she could address it and begin healing. In the past when this would happen she would go into learned helplessness and self-judgment about how she was feeling. She was delighted with her discovery that she had within her the tools to uncover her own unconscious beliefs and to change them.

Ready to evolve?

Exercise: Write down your self-talk. Identify 3 messages that you tell yourself.

Spend some time in contemplation and ask yourself if these messages are true.

CHAPTER 21

DIVINITY

The quality of being divine; divine nature.

*M*y hope is to empower you to become free of conflict. In my practice, I specialize in assisting my clients to empower themselves by becoming free from conflict. In identifying false beliefs, my clients are then able to change their false beliefs so that they can create the circumstances and relationships that they envision for themselves. I assist my clients in bringing their dreams to life. As I have already mentioned, when you have false beliefs you are creating circumstances in your life that run counter to what you truly want.

Ready to evolve?

Write down a familiar feeling and the corresponding belief.

There are four steps that I teach to empower yourself to identify and change false beliefs.

1. *Identify the feeling that you are having right now about your current circumstances, ie., anger, sadness, resentment, grief, regret, loneliness, unworthiness, fear, anxiety, etc.*
2. *If applicable, identify around the time in your life where you started feeling this way, or remember having a similar feeling.*
3. *Identify the relationship and the circumstances that were happening at that time.*
4. *Imagine the belief or beliefs you created as a result of what was happening or what happened.*
5. *If you cannot relate what you are currently experiencing to some time in the past, it may be lodged in your unconscious. When you have buried things for many years they are not as easy to find for yourself without help.*

When you identify the feelings you are having, it assists you in taking responsibility for your thoughts and feelings. When you take responsibility, you are empowering yourself to recognize that you have choice. You have choice to focus on what you are focusing on or to change your focus. It is difficult if we are feeling stuck due to the unconscious to simply shift to the positive. You must first address the unconscious and/or the ego. OR you can learn that you can shift your being-ness out of ego and then you can go more quickly to the state of being you truly are and want to be. If you stay in ego then you need to address the ego until you feel better so that you can be open to deeper shifting.

The essence of life is simple. We make it complicated in our effort to avoid conflict and by creating conflict. We think that the way we have been taught to live our lives or what we taught ourselves based on our conditioning is the right way and anything that deviates from that does not provide us with the assurance we need that we will be happy and loved. Then when it doesn't go exactly as we think it should we do more conflict avoiding or creating by blaming others or circumstances, finding distractions or pushing away our feelings about the way things are, or pushing difficult feelings into our unconscious so we seemingly will not have to deal with it. Unfortunately, we have to deal with it still. "Dealing" with it may come in the form of failed relationships or work its way into our career or financial life, or we may get sick. Many of us have witnessed our parents enter into old age dealing with a variety of health issues. When we do not face or address our problems and inner conflicts that last throughout our lives we can get physically ill as a result of repressed emotions. We have the ability to choose to do things differently even if we have always done things in a certain way. We can stay right where we are even though parts of our "self" are stuck (projecting, blaming, hiding, creating conflicts), we can go deeper into un-knowing, or we can choose the path to awakening and raise our level of consciousness. We can awaken to the truth of who we really are. We are Love, We are Peace, We are all connected. We are not separate even though we think we are. Many masters have written on this subject. Many continue to write on this subject. The message is not new. Even if we do not choose the path of awakening we are still going to be affected by those who are choosing it. The numbers of those who are choosing it is increasing every day and the actions of these folks will have a ripple effect throughout their families and communities. Most folks will be affected one way or another as we continue to increase the consciousness of the planet towards greater peace.

> *"The universe holds its breath as we choose, instant by instant, which pathway to follow; for the universe, the very essence of life itself, is highly conscious. Every act, thought and choice add to a permanent mosaic; our*

decisions ripple through the universe of consciousness to affect the lives of all."

From Power vs. Force
by David Hawkins

We have entered a new era. We are being called to wake up to our own Divinity. We are not here to just merely eek out a living. We are not here to compete with each other for resources. We are not here to "get more" and if we are in God's favor the more we will get. And at the same time, it doesn't have to be difficult. It doesn't have to be difficult to get our physical needs met. We are the ones who have created the "problem" of earning a living. We have created conflicts from our beliefs that things are supposed to look a certain way or happen a certain way. We have created a mess for ourselves but it doesn't have to stay that way. We can shift to a more conscious way of living. We can stay in the life we have right now and ask to be guided to our Divine purpose. We are here to thrive and invite Life to express Life through our thoughts, words and deeds creating heaven on earth.

CHAPTER 22

BEGIN

To proceed to perform the first or earliest part of some action; commence; start.

"I do not need to wait until I become perfect before I love myself. Loving myself is the quickest way to create a wonderful life".

Louise Hay

*I*f you are not sure where to start, start by being kind. Start by stopping any gossip and replace it with gratitude. Start by changing complaints to opportunities to understand people and situations differently. Start by noticing that every one of us is striving to get their needs met in whatever imperfect way they are doing so. Start *by spending some time alone contemplating or writing or some way that works for you to begin understanding what it is you are looking for, what it is you want to create in your life. Make a point to be kind at a moment that you may have felt otherwise. Most important, be kind to yourself. Start your morning with a gratitude practice that includes gratitude for yourself. Most people find being kind to themselves more challenging than being kind to others. If this is the case for you, then this is exactly where you need to not only start but stay. Give yourself credit for how far you have come even if others haven't noticed all that you have done.*

When you judge others, it is yourself that you judge ten times more. Therefore, if you stop judging yourself, it will be much easier to stop judging others. The less you judge, the more opportunity you have to create peace in your household and in your community. You start by creating peace in yourself. You start by accessing the peace that already lives inside of you, that is your birthright. Peace is your true nature. Peace is what you are here to live.

Ready to evolve? Write down the message you receive.

Exercise to start each morning: Begin by taking a few deep breaths breathing in through your nose and out through your mouth. Do the "hook-up" from Eden Energy medicine placing one finger between your eyes and one finger on your belly button. Breathe in through your nose and out through your mouth a few times. Tap your cheek bones several times. If you feel guided: do Donna's Eden's Daily Energy Routine and give yourself a spinal flush. (You can do this for yourself on the corner of a wall if you don't have someone to do it for you).

Ask to connect to higher consciousness or Christ consciousness.

Say to yourself: "I choose to stand in Love, take responsibility, see the Truth, and find and create solutions inside of Love" (from Ashley Lee).

I choose to be in Zero Point.

Then, put your hand on our heart and ask "what would you like me to know today". If there is a specific subject that you would like guidance for focus in on that subject to receive the guidance. Sit in meditation to receive guidance and support for anything you are working on or healing. You may also receive healing at this time.

Pay attention to your body and any aches or pains you have and ask for guidance about what may be asking for attention. You may be guided to a consciousness challenge or a spiritual issue you are currently working on. You can do any of this at any time throughout the day.

If you are waiting for such a time that you deem that you have arrived at a place in yourself where you have done enough, fixed enough, given enough, been good enough, waited enough, or something else before you can begin fully loving yourself then you will never arrive at the right time or place. You can love yourself right where you are. If you could see the truth of your world you would see that what you determined was imperfection was perfection happening for you. When you notice around you, the people, circumstances, opportunities – you allow yourself to awaken to your guidance. When you follow your guidance step by step without attachment you are guided to uncover the best possible advice you could receive. It is your inner guidance that leads you down the path of love in Service to US.

You can learn to listen to yourself when something isn't right for you. This is just as important that you follow your guidance when it tells you that someone or something is not right for you. This is valuable to pay attention to if you doubt your ability to know what is and is not leading you from a place of loving yourself. Sometimes it is unclear if your interest in someone or something is a conscious or an unconscious choice. There are no wrong answers since whatever you choose will provide you with something that you are learning on your path to the best expression of yourself. It just might take longer if you continue to make choices from the unconscious.

Available at our fingertips are tools that are given US to assist in addressing four major aspects of being human: Physical, mental, emotional and spiritual.

When you deepen your innate ability to use your intuition you can use these tools to increase your awareness and awaken conscious relating and conscious living. I have found that I am far less judgmental of myself, others, circumstances and situations as a result of using these methods. I experience consistent joy for the first time in my life as I address these four aspects of my being in relation to myself and in relation to the world. There is more than one way to ignite your intuitive abilities. You may just "know" the answer to questions or you may see or hear the answers to your questions. Others use kinesiology to "test" to get answers to their questions. You can use muscle/energy testing to receive answers about what is going on in your body and in your energy systems. This is not to replace going to see your physician where necessary. The discussion of kinesiology is beyond the scope of this book. It is however a suggested option for "tuning" in to tap into your inner guidance.

When I have an issue I use the "self-test" method and ask my higher self if what is happening is physical, mental, emotional or spiritual. I feel in my body after I receive an answer to see if they both match and if they do not I continue asking until I feel satisfied that I have arrived at the answer. In addition, I use Joe Dispenza's meditation

"The Blessing of the Energy Center's" (on Youtube) to help access a higher state of consciousness. How this meditation works is explained in detail in Joe Dispenza's series on Gaia called "Rewired". I ask questions if I am experiencing something physical which could be anything from indigestion to soreness in my hip, a cold, a broken bone, etc. I first ask if the root cause of what is happening is physical, mental, emotional, or spiritual. I use this same methodology for any discomfort I am experiencing including emotional or situational. Then I refer to one of the following:

When I am self-testing about what is going on with me regarding personal discomfort in my relating to myself or with others or situations and I receive that it is mental or emotional, I refer to the "Consciousness Challenge Toolkit" (leapofconsciousness.com). I ask which number it is and if it is more than one and then I read the relevant ones and meditate on how I am or have created this. I usually feel relief in just reading it once but it is also important to contemplate how I created this from a deeper level. The Toolkit supports you to acknowledge, release and heal your consciousness challenges. When you heal yourself and raise your conscious awareness and conscious relating, you are doing so in Service to Us. It is not just so that you can live the life you want to live because in living the life you dream of others will also see that it is possible for them.

When I use self-testing to assist in intuiting the root cause of the discomfort I am experiencing and I find that it is "Spiritual", I refer to the Gene Keys by Richard Rudd. The Gene Keys are an advanced guide and a tool for finding the answers you seek about the greater meaning in your life. In addition, you don't have to wait to feel psychological or physical pain to ask what you are guided to refer to. You can ask each morning when you ask higher consciousness what it wants you to know today, for which one to refer for what you are currently going through or working on.

You are who you have been looking for. You have all the resources you need inside you. Everything that I have referred to in this book is showing us that you are always connected to the source of Love which is also the source of healing. When you step into your Being-ness you are healed. Your beliefs create your thoughts, your thoughts create your feelings, and your feelings create your actions. If you are creating from unconscious beliefs, thoughts and actions you will not create the life you truly want. If you are creating from conscious beliefs that are not true but that you think are true, you will not create the life you truly want. In your powerful creating, you have the ability to create physical illness AND you have the ability, at the same time, to heal your physical illnesses. The first book I ever read on self-help was by Louise Hay, entitled "You Can Heal Your Life". In this book, Louise introduced us to how our thoughts create our illnesses and how changing those thoughts can heal our illnesses. Donna Eden wrote a book called "Energy Medicine", where she teaches how to heal ourselves through addressing our energy systems.

This book became so popular that Donna started a school to teach people her techniques which came naturally to her through her own abilities. Donna healed herself from a life-threatening illness because she could "see" how energy moves. Donna teaches that you do not have to be able to see the way she does to be able to heal yourself.

> *Everybody on the planet is already a healer because you carry it in your DNA*
> *— Donna Eden*

When I want to address something that is physical, I go to "Energy Medicine". In fact, healing all aspects of ourselves can come from any of these systems. Addressing an issue through "Energy Medicine" can help heal something emotional in nature as well as address a physical aspect of an issue, addressing something through the emotional route can also heal something physical and so on. All of it is connected and interwoven. We need all of us to bring forward our gifts and talents so that everyone has something that speaks to their hearts and minds when they need it. The internet has opened up opportunities to reach people all over the world. This has been helpful to access people from all over the world who are right for you to work with or create community with as well as to discover how many of us are saying the similar things. We are at a critical time and place in the evolution of humanity.

You can learn immediately by watching videos that

are posted on Youtube. There are video's of Donna Eden's Daily Energy Routine that you can learn today that will help you balance your energy systems. It is that fast that you can find resources, learn and heal yourself. When your energy bodies are in balance you are more apt to have less stress and be open to following your inner guidance to your next steps to health, healing, happiness and creating the life you truly want in Service To Us right here, right now. It doesn't have to take time.

I use energy medicine techniques and exercises to bring my energy body and physical body into balance as I continue to upgrade my way of being in the world. As I raise my conscious awareness, I release "dis-ease" in my body in the form of stuck or slow-moving energy as well as energy that is creating dis-ease in my body. I heal diseases before they happen. If something does become physical I can work together with my western medicine doctor to treat what is happening in the physical body, if necessary. I have experienced, on more than one occasion, a Physician telling me that they don't know why I had such severe anemia, recurring pancreatitis, lingering cough that didn't respond to every possible treatment including steroids and breathing treatments and antibiotics and inhalers. I had every possible blood test and scan and scope and nothing showed up to explain why I had these ailments. I healed all of these ailments energetically with the help of energy/quantum healing. I keep my body balanced with daily energy exercises as well as a regular practice of gratitude and I also pay attention to what my body is telling me through aches and pains and tiredness. I consult charts and indexes when I feel guided to do so which also keeps disease from happening in the physical body. I address consciousness challenges at the mental, emotional and spiritual levels through a process of uncovering and changing old beliefs therefore preventing physical manifestations of "dis-eased" thinking and suppressed emotions. Everyone can benefit from energetic support for the shifts and changes that occur while working with the psychological. In addition, ongoing support for your energy body can aid in the overall process of healing. When you feel better your thoughts improve and you find it easier to stand in love instead of fear. When you stand in love instead of fear you can create loving answers for the problems in your life. When you look for solutions while standing in fear you find fearful answers. Love is always present as it flows through everything.

Your body is designed to maintain its health. You are not "supposed" to break down, to get sick, to "age". Your body has ultimate wisdom for health and wellness. It is our minds that create our cells to turn. It is our minds that say that certain things happen when we age and we cannot prevent that. Many of us maintain that belief which keeps it going and therefore we see it in our own bodies. We believe our bodies to break down as a result of aging. You can change this belief and therefore change the way you age. You are the designer of your future. You have freedom of choice. If we look at the past and what happened to those who have come before us we see many who break down with aging but we also have examples of those who did not. Jack Lalane was an example in this country of someone who didn't buy into the program that we have to "age" a certain way. There are also examples of people in other countries who continue to contribute to their families by cooking and taking care of the home or working on the family farm or business well into their "elderly "years. We lose a great natural resource by our elderly citizens stopping contributing their gifts and talents because they are "retired" or are "old" and breaking down. I recently saw on social media a new concept of having a daycare center inside of an assisted living home. This is a brilliant idea on many levels. Seniors have the time and attention that the little ones appreciate. The little ones need to be watched while their parents go to work. In many societies the older generations watch the children while the parents go to work. We have lost much of that in this country as a result of people moving away from extended families for various reasons. We could keep the cost of childcare to a minimum utilizing a natural resource.

When you have a variety of resources in your tool chest you can utilize all of them at once or at different times for total overall health and wellness. It makes it easier to discern what is happening when you have balanced your energy and cleared the energy of others from your energetic bodies. Once you know what is yours, you can get to work addressing what is ready for you. You can give the part of your "self" love that has a belief or a judgement about yourself or others and thank this part of your "self" for being ready to show you something that you get to clear or change. Then using your intuition, ask if what is being shown to you has a "mental, emotional, spiritual or physical" root cause. Then you can intuit if what you are working on is one or more of the consciousness challenges or if it is one or more of the gene keys. Once you decide where to look, you can read about and meditate on what it is in you that is shifting or that got created that you can now choose to change. If you release suppressed emotions, you heal future diseases. You practice preventative medicine by releasing suppressed emotions. Indexes support us in accessing the emotional problems that you have suppressed. It isn't always easy to access what has been suppressed because often people have hidden it from themselves. Sometimes while you are unearthing and addressing suppressed emotions in yourself it is uncomfortable. You can give yourself love and nurturing through your process of releasing suppressed emotions, by supporting yourself using Energy Medicine techniques. This helps you ease into new and improved ways of being in the world, it helps you when you are ill as well as when you are well, it also helps you to balance the flow of your energy as well as heal your physical body. You have everything you need available to you and within you. If you don't have what you need right now ask your higher self to guide you to what will help you with what you need. There is also information in asking yourself what you want. What you want is guiding you to your next step. If there is discomfort in you regarding what you want then that is information for you that you can assess by using your intuition to guide you to the root cause and then to utilizing one of the charts.

When you are willing to look at the truth in you and around you, you can do something about it. Many of us do not realize that we hide the truth from ourselves. Learning about your consciousness challenges is a gentle way of revealing to you what you have hidden within. Problems that you have in your life reveal consciousness challenges that you can address when you ask yourself what is happening that is creating this "problem" that you are experiencing. Having a guide is often helpful in cases where you have hidden things from your "self." It is difficult to know what you have hidden because it often doesn't make linear or rational sense. Sometimes you have inherited something from a family line therefore you wouldn't readily know when something of this nature is affecting you. If you know to ask about it to your higher self you can access the information. The more you practice listening to your higher self the easier it gets. Like anything, it takes practice. In practicing you learn when you are in fear and creating solutions based in fear and when you are in love and creating solutions based in love. It is important to ask your higher self if your unconscious is creating solutions based in fear. As you grow and change your conscious awareness we may still have unconscious fear in certain areas of your life even if you have made conscious changes in those areas. You learn to fine tune your "looking" when you learn about the possibilities. Your conscious mind can be doing one thing while your unconscious is doing another. Sitting down in contemplation or focused meditation will help you to practice what you are learning. When you access unconscious beliefs, it is important to meditate on how they were created. When you understand how your beliefs were created, they are easier to change.

You may feel wobbly at first when stepping out of your comfort zone and into a new place of following inner guidance. It is important that you not judge or project on others, especially when they are going through a transformation and making changes that you may not understand. It is a new way of doing things when you take a leap of faith and choose to have trust and faith in the presence of the unknown. We are all sensitive beings and can feel the projections or judgments of others even if they are half way across the world. Projections can slow or impede the progress of those who are being projected upon. Judgments can be felt which makes it especially important when someone is already experiencing self-doubt because they are changing old patterns. We all need to support each other on our journeys. When we stand and project, "What is she doing?", "Where is this going?" from a place of doubt or fear, this can hold a person back or cause them to feel distress in the midst of their leap of faith. A leap of faith requires just that, faith. It means that a different way of operating in the world, outside of the perceived security in the old paradigm, is going to look different both to the person making personal changes and to those around them. "What do you mean you are quitting your job and you don't have a new one?". This would be an example of stepping out of perceived security and into trust and faith, if you are taking guided action to, for example, quit your job so that you can focus on creating inside of your life purpose. This is not to recommend that everyone quits their job to find their life purpose but it may be something that someone could be guided to do so that they have time to focus on creating the new. What may also come if you are guided to do this is finding that each month the bills get paid after opening to new solutions to which you weren't previously open or aware.

CHAPTER 23

INTUITION

*Direct perception of truth, fact, etc.,
independent of reasoning process;
immediate apprehension.*

*W*hat is your gift that you bring the world? Your gift is your "superpower". What is that one thing that you do well or you have always wanted to do? Whether or not you are doing it now, it is there. Your energy goes up when you are in the presence of it. It gets your attention and beckons you. You have beyond a doubt something that is unique to you. I always knew what I wanted to do. In high school I told my friends that I was going to be a psychologist even though at the time I didn't have good grades or much like school. I had my own consciousness challenges which I would not unravel until my late 40's and early 50's. My energy went up on the subject of Psychology and self-help. I was always interested in what made people do the things they did. I spent many years looking for what "works" in the field of healing and for a time felt that psychology was not helpful. I explored many forms of energy and spiritual healing and finally realized that there is not one way or one person (Guru consciousness) that is the solution. I incorporated what I learned in my own healing creating my version of energetic psychology. Everything I do with my clients I have done and received the benefits of myself. My life is my laboratory and my healing the results and the proof. My practice has also been my laboratory. As soon as I learn something new I bring it to my practice. My clients are the gauge for how something works for more than just myself and I am able to fine tune how I work with others based on the first-hand experiences with clients.

My super power is helping people on the path of awakening through uncovering what is unconscious. I see, sense and feel unconscious beliefs and patterns in others. When I decided I wanted to go into the field of Psychology I had no idea what was going to come from it. I also stepped away from it for a while to explore other methods of healing which proved to be an important part of uncovering my gifts. I didn't know where my exploring was going but knew that I felt my energy go up learning about and participating in energy healing as well as taking classes and reading books on the subject. I followed what

I "wanted" and what felt good to me. I didn't have a clear plan and was still looking for answers for my own healing. When I set out to do things that were a part of my calling, things just worked out. The help showed up at the right time, the money to pay for it came, and the time to do it was opened up. I am not "done" finding my gifts. Our gifts continue to unfold as we follow our guidance in Service to Us.

I was guided to the 57ᵗʰ Gene Key. I had a small red patch under my left eye and I asked my inner guidance what this was. I received that it was spiritual and was guided to the gene keys book and felt strongly that I needed to add this to my book. The following is an excerpt from the chapter – the 57ᵗʰ Gift in support of all of us being guided to connect with and utilize our innate gift of intuition.

The 57ᵗʰ Gift – Intuition

Of all the 64 Gene Keys, few have such a profound connection to individual human health as this 57ᵗʰ Gene Key. As the foundational aspect of the Ring of Matter, the 57ᵗʰ Gene Key governs the cycle of gestation, which in turn lays the pattern for your development throughout childhood. It is during this primary cycle that all your genetic programming is laid down. Your genes build your body at the frequency of the energetic field in which your mother lives. Therefore, every mother plays a crucial role in the biological, emotional and mental structure of the child. The other is actually a co-creator of the incarnating child, every thought, feeling and impulse running through her being will direct the DNA within the foetus. This obviously puts a huge responsibility on pregnant mothers and has significant implications concerning the transformation of our species through deep honouring of the mother and of the importance of her role during pregnancy.

The developing foetus lives in a world of frequency. It literally swims in and imbibes the tones, colours, sounds, emotions, thought and intentions of its environment. Even so, the foetus interprets these frequencies through the mother's responses to them. Thus the mother's frequency directly dictates the destiny of the future human being. Each of the three trimesters of pregnancy relate to the three seven year cycles of the child's development, the first being the physical, the second the emotional and the third the mental. In other words, in those first nine months, the first 21 years of your life are completely mapped out. Of course, no one is entirely a victim of the frequency of their mother. At any stage in any of the developmental cycles issues rise to the surface in order that they may be embraced, purified and healed. As your own frequency rises, so you will gradually heal the many layers of your inner being. Even so, it is important to realise how great a head start a child can get from elevated frequencies in the mother during pregnancy.

The 57ᵗʰ Gift of Intuition is basically your body's system for interacting harmoniously with the outer world. It is the low-frequency prenatal programming that later interferes with the clear operation of your intuition. Although all illnesses were imprinted during the gestation cycle, they can be healed through directly raising the frequency of your DNA. This essentially resets or reboots your entire genetic operating system. As you address the Shadow states that such a process naturally brings to light, so you will witness a deepening sensitivity inside you to everything and everyone in the world around you. This is what the 57th Gift of Intuition is about – it is the natural guidance system of all human beings.

If you review the evolution of human awareness up until our present point in time, you may discover the vital insight on which our future evolution will hinge. This insight concerns the role of the inner masculine and inner feminine principles. If we go back in our evolution to primitive man, we can see how deeply developed was our instinctive awareness – our gut feeling or hunch. Our individual survival depended on the innate animal instinct functioning through our bodies, i.e. through the five primary senses and the mythical sixth sense – that ability to perceive something coming before our physical senses actually detect it. All human beings alive today have inherited this inner sixth sense if we but knew how to trust in it. In a word, your most powerful inner compass is your intuition.

Having developed our intuition – the feminine aspect of our psyche – humanity then went on to develop its masculine side, the mind. Whereas intuition listen and receives, mind explores and conquers. This is why our current epoch is so fascinating. We human beings must now remember our past and reconnect to the power of our intuition. Having done this, we will have to learn to trust our intuition over and above our mental faculties. In this way, we will create a naturally structured internal psyche that mirrors nature. Intuition is how nature talks to and through human beings – it is the auditory canal through which the whole coordinates and communicates with its many parts. If we humans can attune ourselves to this gentle, subtler internal voice, we will finally begin to feel physically at ease. Furthermore, when our internal hierarchy is naturally formulated in this way, the genius of the mind can finally come into play and follow the dictates of nature herself.

The human mind is a truly extraordinary instrument. It is also a very dangerous instrument without the proper internal guidance. We can all see how destructive the mind can be when it is allowed free range without the sense of being connected to the whole. As humanity learns once again to trust its deeper feminine side, as it is beginning to do, the mind will naturally fall into its own rhythm. This revolution is already underway in the individual. Intuition emerges from the whole so it naturally leads to synthesis, and intuition backed by the intellect is capable of extraordinary things. The fact is that the more you trust in your intuition, the more integrated your life becomes. Your relationships open up and become softer, the path of your destiny is made increasingly clear and events move more smoothly, as though the entire universe were supporting you. This of course exactly what is occurring.

The process of learning to again trust in your intuition is nothing less than the dismantling of the illusion that you are separate from life. It is a return to the heightened sensitivity you had in your mother's womb. The more you widen this pathway inside yourself, the easier life becomes. Your fear and your anxiety will persist in the beginning, but after some time intuition will become more natural and powerful inside you, as though an invisible force were overriding your old conditioned programming. Furthermore, every time you trust in your intuition, or make a decision based on it, you raise the frequency of your whole aura. Your awareness operating system changes gear and your body hums with life. The deeper you go into this new awareness the more fear inside is transcended. At higher levels still, you will begin to sense vibrations through your whole body. One of the great revelations you may have through the 57th Gift is that fear is not inside you. It is a field that you may live in, pass through or ascend beyond. Evolving your so-called sixth sense is the first stage in this process of vibratory ascension because it allows you to access the universal quantum field or collective unconscious.

Once your body becomes lighter and vibrates at higher frequencies, you enter an amazing world known by many names in different traditions. This the world of the gods

*and goddesses, or what theosophists call the causal plane.
One this level the higher mind begins to function, although
it has little in common with the mind as we experience
it at lower frequencies. The nature of the higher mind is
clairaudience – the ability to pick up vibrations through
your aura and interpret them through your brain. It is
from this causal plane or synfield that all great revelations
occur at various frequency bands with the Gift level itself,
and the purity of the messages depends on the frequency
of the aura that is receiving them. However, the higher
you go up the spectrum of frequency, the more integrative
and synthesized the transmissions become. In the end
however, regardless of the potential heights that this Gift
offers human beings, this 57th Gift of Intuition shows you
one of the clearest and simplest paths to move beyond the
shadows of your fears. ("Gene Keys" pages 462-464, by
Richard Rudd)*

*There is no one way to do this. Each individual life,
while weaving its tapestry, will be met with what they
need in the next step of their evolution. If you choose to be
open-minded about this process it will unfold with greater
ease and flow. If you choose to be in resistance you will be
given the experiences and opportunities you need for your
growth all the same. You will continue to be met with what
you are choosing to create, as you are a powerful creator,
which will be based on our conscious and unconscious
beliefs. When you live your life in conscious awareness*

what is available to you is limitless. My wish for all of us is that we bring into our awareness that there is more. We don't know what we don't know which sometimes seems cruel to me as I witness the suffering of another. Let us all recognize that every one of us is just trying to get their needs met and at the core of every personal want and desire is the longing to come home and the longing for love.

BIBLIOGRAPHY

(2003). In Merriam-Webster's dictionary (11ᵗʰ ed.). Springfield, MA: Merriam-Webster Dictionary

Dispenza, Joe. "Rewired" Series on Gaia; The Blessing of the Energy Centers Meditation. Youtube.

Eden, Donna. (1998). "Energy Medicine." New York: TarcherPerigree.

Francis,., Ferri, G., & Sala, E. (2013). The Prayer of St. Francis.

Gladwell, M. (2000). "The Tipping Point: How Little Things Can Make a Big Difference." Boston: Little, Brown.

Hawkins, David Dr. (2014). "Power vs. Force." Carlsbad: Hay House.

Francis,., Ferri, G., & Sala, E. (2013). The Prayer of St. Francis.

Luftenegger, Paul.

Rudd, Richard. (2013, 2015) "Gene Keys: Unlocking The Higher Purpose Hidden In Your DNA." London: Watkins Publishing.

Silverstein, Shel. (1996). "Falling Up" New York: Harper Collins.

Solt, A., Egan, S., & Ono, Y. (1988). Imagine: John Lennon. New York: Macmillan Pub.

Teresa, M., & Kolodiejchuk, B. (2007). Mother Teresa: Come be my light : the private writings of the "Saint of Calcutta". New York: Doubleday.

Williamson, Marianne. (1976). "A Course in Miracles." New York: Viking.

CPSIA information can be obtained
at www.ICGtesting.com
Printed in the USA
BVHW071919030221
599237BV00002B/307

9 781982 261269